Write first 1

Progression in cross-curricular writing skills

Ray Barker
Christine Moorcroft

First published in 2001 by:

Nelson Thornes
Delta Place
27 Bath Road
CHELTENHAM GL53 7TH
United Kingdom

01 02 03 04 15 / 10 9 8 7 6 5 4 3 2 1

A catalogue record for this book is available from the British Library.

ISBN 0 7487 6148 9

Developed and produced by Start to Finish
Typeset by Paul Manning
Printed and bound in Spain by Graficas Estella S.A.

Acknowledgements

Unit 1: William Saroyan, 'The First Day of School', from *Little Children* (Faber & Faber), reprinted by permission of Laurence Pollinger Ltd, the William Saroyan Foundation and the Stanford University Libraries; **Unit 2:** from Dylan Thomas, *Portrait of the Artist as a Young Dog* (Everyman, 1993), reprinted by permission of David Higham Asssociates Ltd; **Unit 5:** weather charts from Teletext Weather website, reprinted by permission of Teletext Ltd; **Unit 7:** from Plantagenet Somerset Fry, *Kings and Queens: a Royal History of England and Scotland* (Dorling Kindersley, 1990), © 1990 Dorling Kindersley, reprinted by permission of the publisher; from Christopher Lee, *This Sceptred Isle* (BBC Books, 1997), © Christopher Lee, 1996, reprinted by permission of BBC Worldwide Ltd; from Magnus Magnusson, *Scotland: The Story of a Nation* (HarperCollins, 2000), reprinted by permission of the author; **Unit 8:** from Ian McEwan, *The Daydreamer* (Jonathan Cape, 1994), reprinted by permission of The Random House Group Ltd; from Russell Hoban, *Turtle Diary* (Jonathan Cape, 1975), reprinted by permission of David Higham Associates Ltd; **Unit 10:** from Alan Garner, 'Thursday's Child' from *Elidor* (William Collins, 1980), reprinted by permission of HarperCollllins Publishers; **Unit 11:** from Roald Dahl, *Boy: Tales of Childhood* (Jonathan Cape, 1984), reprinted by permission of David Higham Associates Ltd; **Unit 14:** Esther Addley, 'Highway panic as snake legs it to freedom' from *The Guardian* (18 October 2000), reprinted by permission of the publisher; **Unit 17:** Michael Bateman, 'The Plumber' from *Story: The Second Book*, edited by David Jackson and Dennis Pepper (Penguin Education, 1973), © H.M. Bateman Designs Ltd, reproduced by kind permission of H.M. Bateman Designs Ltd; **Unit 20:** advertisement for Aquamark Steam Cleaner reprinted by permission of Health & Home Shoppping Ltd, artwork by Lavery Rowe Advertising Ltd; text from advertisement for Chicken O's from *Voilà* magazine, reprinted by permission of Bird's Eye Wall's Ltd; **Unit 22:** The Chocolate Experience 1999 leaflet reprinted by permission of Cadbury World.

Every effort has been made to trace or contact all copyright holders. The publishers would be pleased to rectify any omissions brought to their notice at the earliest opportunity.

Contents

Describing

1	Describing experiences	4
2	Describing people	8
3	Describing places	10
4	Describing things: a classic novel	13
5	Describing things: the weather	15
6	Describing processes	17
7	Making notes: mapping out ideas	20

Narrating

8	Point of view	22
9	Narrators	26
10	Dialogue	29
11	Autobiography	32
12	Making notes: planning a biography	35

Recounting and explaining

13	Explanations	38
14	Newspaper reports	40
15	Reference texts: the Internet	42
16	Giving directions	45
17	Planning and sequencing	48
18	Making notes: charts and diagrams	51

Arguing

19	Making notes: for and against	54
20	Persuasive language	57
21	Speeches	60
22	Leaflets	63

1 Describing experiences

This is a short story from America.

He was a little boy named Jim, the first and only child of Dr Louis Davy, 717 Mattei Building, and it was his first day at school. His father was French, a small heavy-set man of forty whose boyhood had been full of poverty and unhappiness and ambition. His mother was dead: she died when Jim was born, and the only woman he knew intimately was Amy, the Swedish housekeeper.

It was Amy who dressed him in his Sunday clothes and took him to school. Jim liked Amy, but he didn't like her for taking him to school. He told her so. All the way to school he told her so.

I don't like you, he said. I don't like you any more.

I like *you*, the housekeeper said.

Then why are you taking me to school? he said.

He had taken walks with Amy before, once all the way to the Court House Park for the Sunday afternoon band concert, but this walk to school was different.

What for? he said.

Everybody must go to school, the housekeeper said.

Did you go to school? he said.

No, said Amy.

Then why do I have to go? he said.

You will like it, said the housekeeper.

He walked on with her in silence, holding her hand. I don't like you, he said. I don't like you any more.

I like you, said Amy.

Then why are you taking me to school? he said again. Why?

The housekeeper knew how frightened a little boy could be about going to school.

You will like it, she said. I think you will sing songs and play games.

I don't want to, he said.

I will come and get you every afternoon, she said.

I don't like you, he told her again.

She felt unhappy about the little boy going to school, but she knew he would have to go.

The school building was very ugly to her and to the boy. She didn't like the way it made her feel, and going up the steps with him she wished he didn't have to go to school. The halls and rooms scared her, and him, and the smell of the place too. And he didn't like Mr Barber, the principal.

Amy despised Mr Barber.

What is the name of your son? Mr Barber said.

This is Dr Louis Davy's son, said Amy. His name is Jim. I am Dr Davy's housekeeper.

James? said Mr Barber.

Not James, said Amy, just Jim.

All right, said Mr Barber. Any middle name?

No, said Amy. He is too small for a middle name. Just Jim Davy.

All right, said Mr Barber. We'll try him

out in the first grade. If he doesn't get along all right we'll try him out in kindergarten.

Dr Davy said to start him in the first grade, said Amy. Not kindergarten.

All right, said Mr Barber.

The housekeeper knew how frightened the little boy was, sitting in the chair, and she tried to let him know how much she loved him and how sorry she was about everything. She wanted to say something fine to him about everything, but she couldn't say anything, and she was very proud of the nice way he got down from the chair and stood beside Mr Barber, waiting to go with him into the classroom.

On the way home she was so proud of him she began to cry.

Miss Binney, the teacher of the first grade, was an old lady who was all dried out. The room was full of little boys and girls. School smelled strange and sad. He sat at a desk and listened carefully.

He heard some of the names: Charles, Alvin, Norman, Betty, Hannah, Juliet, Viola, Polly.

He listened carefully and heard Miss Binney say, Hannah Winter, what *are* you chewing? And he saw Hannah Winter blush. He liked Hannah Winter right from the beginning.

Gum, said Hannah.

Put it in the waste-basket, said Miss Binney.

He saw the little girl walk to the front of the class, take the gum from her mouth, and drop it into the waste-basket.

And he heard Miss Binney say, Ernest Gaskin, what are *you* chewing?

Gum, said Ernest .

And he liked Ernest Gaskin, too.

They met in the schoolyard, and Ernest taught him a few jokes.

Amy was in the hall when school ended. She was sullen and angry at everybody until she saw the little boy. She was amazed that he wasn't changed, that he wasn't hurt, or perhaps utterly unalive, murdered. The

school and everything about it frightened her very much. She took his hand and walked out of the building with him, feeling angry and proud.

Jim said, What comes after twenty-nine?

Thirty, said Amy.

Your face is dirty, he said.

His father was very quiet at the supper table.

What comes after twenty-nine? the boy said.

Thirty, said his father.

Your face is dirty, he said.

In the morning he asked his father for a nickel.

What do you want a nickel for? his father said.

Gum, he said.

His father gave him a nickel and on the way to school he stopped at Mrs Riley's store and bought a package of Spearmint.

Do you want a piece? he asked Amy.

Do you want to give me a piece? the housekeeper asked.

Jim thought about it for a moment, and then said, Yes.

Do you like me? said the housekeeper.

I like you, said Jim. Do you like me?

Describing experiences

Yes, said the housekeeper.

Do you like school?

Jim didn't know for sure, but he knew he liked the part about gum. And Hannah Winter. And Ernest Gaskin.

I don't know, he said.

Do you sing? asked the housekeeper.

No, we don't sing, he said.

Do you play games? she said.

Not in the school, he said. In the yard we do.

He liked the part about the gum very much.

Miss Binney said, Jim Davy, what are you *chewing*?

Ha ha ha, he thought.

Gum, he said.

He walked to the waste-basket and back to his seat, and Hannah Winter saw him, and Ernest Gaskin too. That was the best part of school.

It began to grow too.

Ernest Gaskin, he shouted in the schoolyard, *what* are you *chewing*?

Raw elephant meat, said Ernest Gaskin. Jim Davy, what are *you* chewing?

Jim tried to think of something very funny to be chewing, but he couldn't.

Gum, he said, and Ernest Gaskin laughed louder than Jim laughed when Ernest Gaskin said raw elephant meat.

It was funny no matter what you said.

Going back to the classroom Jim saw Hannah Winter in the hall.

Hannah Winter, he said, *What in the world* are you *chewing*?

The little girl was startled. She wanted to say something nice that would honestly show how nice she felt about Jim saying her name and asking her a funny question, making fun of school, but she couldn't think of anything that nice to say because they were almost in the room and there wasn't time enough.

Tutti-frutti, she said with desperate haste.

It seemed to Jim that he had never before heard such a glorious word, and he kept repeating the word to himself all day.

Tutti-frutti, he said to Amy on the way home.

Amy Larson, he said, *What, are, you, chewing*?

He told his father all about it at the supper table.

He said, Once there was a hill. On the hill there was a mill. Under the mill there was a walk. Under the walk there was a key. What is it?

I don't know, said his father. What is it?

Milwaukee, said the boy.

The housekeeper was delighted.

Mill, Walk, Key, Jim said.

Tutti-frutti.

What's that? said his father.

Gum, he said. The kind Hannah Winter chews.

Who's Hannah Winter? said his father.

She's in my room, he said.

Oh, said his father.

After supper he sat on the floor with the small red and blue and yellow top and hummed while it spinned. It was all right, he guessed. It was still very sad, but the gum part of it was very funny and the Hannah Winter part very nice. Raw elephant meat, he thought with great inward delight.

Raw elephant meat, he said aloud to his father who was reading the evening paper. His father folded the paper and sat on the floor beside him. The housekeeper saw them together on the floor and for some reason tears came to her eyes.

The First Day of School by William Saroyan

Glossary

Mill, Walk, Key Milwaukee, a city in the state of Michigan

Read on!

1 How did you feel about your first day at this school? Complete the chart:

What happened	What I felt about it and why

2 What do you find strange about the way this passage is written?

3 How old is the child? How does the way this story is written give you an impression of this?

4 What details in the story give you the impression of the way a young child thinks?

5 How does the child's attitude to school change throughout the story? What makes him change his attitude?

6 What evidence is there to show that the first day at school changed the relationship between father and son?

Write on!

1 Copy and complete the chart with details from the extract. This will enable you to understand the structure of the story.

2 Write about your first day at school as a young child, using the passage as a model. It can be based on real happenings or can be imaginary.
   • Write about what happened, but also explain how you felt and why.
   • How did you react to events? Remember you are a young child in this activity.

   • Describe people you met and use speech to make them come alive for your reader.

Structure	Details
Some details about the main character	
Going to school and feelings about this	
The school and the teachers – first reactions	
In the classroom	
Making friends – meeting others	
Back home and your reactions	

Over to you!

Use the same format to write about your first day in a new job. This might be a weekend or holiday job. It can be real or imaginary. Use the Activity Sheet to help you plan the content of your writing:

• Use small details which will be of interest to the reader – about the place, people or job.
• Record the events of the day.

• Think about the people you met and what they were like – what they looked like and how they behaved.
• Write about your reactions to events throughout the day. Did your attitudes change?
• Show how you felt about people, places and events. Did they change through the day?

2 Describing people

This extract from Dylan Thomas' autobiography tells of a visit to his grandfather's house.

In the middle of the night I woke from a dream full of whips, lariats as long as serpents, and runaway coaches on mountain passes, and wide, windy gallops over cactus fields, and I heard the old man in the next room crying, 'Gee-up!' and 'Whoa!' and trotting his tongue on the roof of his mouth.

It was the first time I had stayed in grandpa's house. The floorboards had creaked like mice as I climbed into bed, and the mice between the walls had creaked like wood as though another visitor was walking on them. It was a mild summer night, but curtains had flapped and branches beaten against the window. I had pulled the sheets over my head, and soon was roaring and riding in a book.

'Whoa there, my beauties!' cried grandpa. His voice sounded very young and loud, and his tongue had powerful hooves, and he made his bedroom into a great meadow. I thought I would see if he was ill, or had set the bedclothes on fire, for my mother had said that he lit his pipe under the blankets, and had warned me to run to his help if I smelt smoke in the night. I went on tiptoe through the darkness to his bedroom door, brushing against the furniture and upsetting a candlestick with a thump. When I saw there was a light in the room I felt frightened, and as I opened the door I heard grandpa shout, 'Gee-up!' as loudly as a bull with a megaphone.

He was sitting straight up in bed and rocking from side to side as though the bed were on a rough road; the knotted edges of the counterpane were his reins; his invisible horses stood in a shadow beyond the bedside candle. Over a white flannel nightshirt he was wearing a red waistcoat with walnut-size brass buttons. The over-filled bowl of his pipe smouldered among his whiskers like a little burning hayrick on a stick. At the sight of me his hands dropped from the reins and lay blue and quiet, the bed stopped still on a level road, he muffled his tongue into silence, and the horses drew softly up.

'Is there anything the matter, grandpa?' I asked, though the clothes were not on fire. His face in the candlelight looked like a ragged quilt pinned upright on the black air and patched all over with goat-beards.

He stared at me mildly. Then he blew down his pipe, scattering the sparks and making a high, wet dog-whistle of the stem, and shouted: 'Ask no questions.'

After a pause, he said slyly: 'Do you ever have nightmares, boy?'

I said: 'No.'

'Oh, yes, you do,' he said.

I said I was woken by a voice that was shouting to horses.

'What did I tell you?' he said. 'You eat too much. Who ever heard of horses in a bedroom?'

He fumbled under his pillow, brought out a small, tinkling bag, and carefully untied its strings. He put a sovereign in my hand, and said: 'Buy a cake.' I thanked him and wished him goodnight.

As I closed my bedroom door, I heard his voice crying loudly and gaily, 'Gee-up! Gee-up!' And the rocking of the travelling bed.

from *Portrait of the Artist as a Young Dog*
by Dylan Thomas

Glossary

lariat lasso

Read on!

1 Why is the boy surprised when he wakes up?
2 What is actually happening in the house?
3 What is the house like? What details make it easily imaginable?
4 What has the boy been told about the old man by his mother? How would this make the boy feel about him?
5 How does the old man persuade the boy he has not seen the strange events?

Detail	How it made me feel about him

6 Copy the chart and record three pieces of detail about grandpa and what it tells you:
7 How does your attitude towards him change by the end?

Write on!

1 When you describe characters, you do not simply describe their physical appearance. Copy and complete the chart with information from the extract. In the last box, write what you have learned about this character.

2 Dylan Thomas is very skilled at creating images which enable the reader easily to imagine things. Use the Activity Sheet to record these and say how they work.

Image	The impression it gives me
Trotting his tongue on the roof of his mouth	
Floorboards creaked like mice	
Mice creaked like wood ... as if another visitor were walking on them	

Over to you!

Write a description of an old person whom you find in unusual circumstances and who surprises you.

• Use the same structure as Dylan Thomas – you could use the ending as a model.

• Remember to use careful details and images to create a picture of the character in your reader's mind.

You could look closely at the person's face and describe its various parts: its shape, eyes, nose, ears, hair.

3   Describing places

In this extract from an autobiographical novel, Penelope Lively returns to Egypt, where she spent her childhood, and looks for the house in which she once lived.

We reached the railway line. The level crossing was automated now. Was this the place at which we used to sit in the car, waiting for the anticipated arrival of the eventual interminable passage of a goods train? We would be there for half an hour, sometimes, slotted into a long impatient line of carts and trucks, with those who could hooting continuously, others bawling at the signalmen, and anyone on foot climbing over the barrier and crawling under the train, which was frequently stationary. I studied the new, efficient-looking arrangement and suddenly it came to me that just beyond the railway line there should be a canal, and indeed there was. But now the road curved off to the right in a way that

seemed to me wrong. There was a sea of shabbily built apartment blocks on all sides, balconies festooned with washing, the street strewn with rubble, people everywhere, children running around like puppies, more of the same visible down every alley. I began to feel like a time traveller, seeing still the white-dappled clover fields and the waving sugar cane.

Definitely, the road was going too far to the right. We stopped the taxi and the driver did some astute thinking and vanished into a coffee-house to see if he could find some old men who would remember this area way back and who might know if there were still any large old houses surviving. He returned, triumphant. Yes, someone had said there were houses that used to belong to English people, but not down this road, which was built in 1970. Over to the left. Down that way … Vague gesturing.

We set off again, plunging now down pot-holed side roads, the taxi moving amid the rubble at a walking pace. We began to acquire an interesting following. Passers-by interrogated the taxi driver. The news of our mission spread and the following increased. We acquired a man wearing a suit and carrying a briefcase – an incongruous figure in these parts – who offered to act as escort. We were now seven in a taxi. At every street junction – if they could be called that – the driver stopped once more. Conversations were held. People pointed in various directions. Others shook their heads dismissively. We were all by now hot and tired.

And then someone said positively: 'Down there…' The street indicated was wider than most, but so ferociously pot-

railings with a gate at which appeared a *gaffir*, who opened up at once with broad smiles when all was explained. The house was now the administrative offices of a technical school, apparently – and there in what had once been our garden were the concrete block-houses which were the workshops and classrooms. But it was the lunch hour and there was no one around. We trooped into the precincts, all fifty of us, and I led a sort of royal progress round the outside of the house, taking photographs, while the founder members of the entourage explained to latecomers what it was about. The man with the briefcase presided benignly, as if it had all been his doing. Everyone shook hands with everyone else. It was not possible to go inside because it was locked up. I didn't really want to anyway. This was quite enough. The *gaffir* had been associated with the place for long enough to know something of the past. He launched on an explanation to our companion interpreter, pointing to an open space filled with rubbish, cats and playing children – and as he pointed I saw a rectangle of razed concrete walling, with a shallow pit alongside it, like archaeological remains. The fragments of our swimming-pool and the engine-house in which lived our electricity generator.

holed that it seemed wise to take to our feet. We walked a hundred yards or so, escorted by our entourage which had swollen to twenty or thirty. And there suddenly was a large, very dilapidated house which certainly had a whiff of familiarity. A pillared porch, green shutters … But it didn't seem right. I studied it. Everyone else watched me, expectantly. 'No,' I said unhappily, 'I don't think it is.'

We continued. Beyond the building was a newish mosque surrounded by tenements. And then a bit of waste ground and then … There it was. Bulaq Dakhrur. Standing there battered but alive, the old shutters still on most of the windows, the big veranda at the back, the front porch, the whole infinitely familiar outline that has featured in my dreams for forty years. I said, 'This is it.'

Beaming smiles all round. My companions emotional. The entourage congratulating each other, and me. The first house we came to, I now realised, had been that of our neighbours. The middle house of the three had been replaced by the mosque. And Bulaq Dakhrur stood isolated, fenced off behind

Of the surroundings, everything had gone. The fields, the village, the palm-fringed canals. Our garden, with its thirty-foot eucalyptus trees, the lawns, the ponds, the pergolas. Nothing left but the house, stolidly clinging on. Somehow, this was not sad but curiously exhilarating. I had not expected it to be there at all. And now the building seemed to have the dignity of the Sphinx, which looks aloofly out over the degradation all around.

from *Oleander, Jacaranda* by Penelope Lively

Read on!

1 How do you know what kind of country you are in right from the start of the extract?
2 How do other people help the author to find her old home?
3 Point out two ways in which the author makes the place and buildings come alive for the reader right from the first paragraph.
4 How do her feelings change throughout the description?
5 Why do you think there are so many short sentences in this description?
6 Copy the chart and list the stages in finding the author's childhood home. This will show you the structure of the piece of writing.

Stage 1	In a taxi by herself looking for the house.
Stage 2	Others try to help her out and ask questions
Stage 3	
Stage 4	

Write on!

1 Use the Activity Sheet to complete the charts with information from the passage. This will show you how detail is important in describing places.
2 Imagine you are looking for your own home in twenty years' time. Write about how you found it and what it looks like now. Follow the structure of this extract:
   • Looking for a place from your past.
   • A group of people helps you.
   • You find it after some false starts, and recognise it.

How to describe a place:

Shapes	
Sizes	
Colours	
Textures	

Using your senses:

What do I see?	
What do I hear?	
What do I smell?	

Over to you!

Describe the place in the passage from the point of view of the man with the briefcase. He will see the same things, but they will appear differently to him – he lives in the city, this is not his childhood home.

• Follow the same structure, from when he joins the search.
• Use detail from the passage and explain how he would feel and react to the search.
• Use speech to make the scene come more alive.

4 Describing things: a classic novel

In this extract from a classic novel, Pip, the young boy in the story, has stolen some food, including a pork pie, in order to help an escaped convict who is hiding in the marshes.

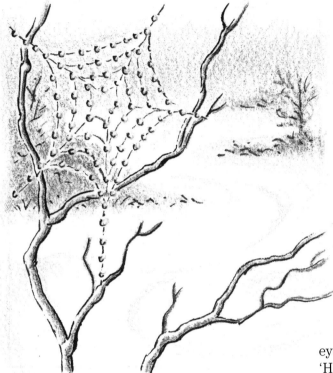

It was a rimy morning, and very damp. I had seen the damp lying on the outside of my little window, as if some goblin had been crying here all night and using the window for a pocket handkerchief. Now I saw the damp lying on the bare hedges and spare grass, like a coarser sort of spiders' webs; hanging itself from twig to twig and blade to blade. On every rail and gate, wet lay clammy, and the marsh mist was so thick that the wooden finger on the post directing people to our village – a direction which they never accepted, for they never came there – was invisible to me until I was quite close under it. Then, as I looked up at it, while it dripped, it seemed to my oppressed conscience like a phantom devoting me to the Hulks.

The mist was heavier yet when I got out upon the marshes, so that instead of my running at everything, everything seemed to run at me. This was very disagreeable to a guilty mind. The gates and dykes and banks came bursting at me through the mist, as if they cried plainly as could be: 'A boy with Somebody-else's pork pie! Stop him!'

The cattle came upon me with like suddenness, staring out of their eyes, and steaming out of their nostrils. 'Holloa, young thief!' One black ox, with a white cravat on – who even had to my awakened conscience something of a clerical air – fixed me so obstinately with his eyes, and moved his blunt head round in such an accusatory manner as I moved round that I blubbered out to him: 'I couldn't help it, sir! It wasn't for myself I took it!' Upon which he put down his head, blew a cloud of smoke out of his nose, and vanished with a kick-up of his hind-legs and a flourish of his tail.

from *Great Expectations* by Charles Dickens

Glossary

rimy frosty
Hulks prison ships used to transport people to Australia in the nineteenth century

Read on!

In this extract, the weather plays an important part in the description. It gives us an idea of how the character feels.

1   Copy and complete the chart to identify important details:

	Details which tell me
What time of day is it?	
What is the weather like?	
Where is the boy?	
How do we know he has committed a crime?	
How does he feel about his crime?	

2   Find evidence from the detail and language of the passage to show that it was written more than a hundred years ago.

Write on!

1   The writer uses personification – he makes things come alive – to show you how the weather affects the character. How does this give you a clearer impression of how the boy felt? Use the Activity Sheet to help you with this activity.

2   Imagine that you feel guilty about something you have done. The world around you seems to know about your crime and to come to life. How does this happen and make you feel worse? Write a paragraph about walking home alone at night in the mist. Use some of these ideas to help you:

- **Sounds** – a dripping gutter, echoes of your footsteps
- **Sights** – fog or mist hiding things, your shadow, reflections of passing traffic, branches of trees moving in the wind, sharp railings silhouetted against the sky
- **Feelings** – cobwebs brushing against your face, damp mist clinging to you, water running down your face.

Over to you!

1   Imagine a desert scene. Copy this chart and use it to help you create detail:

Feature	Details	The effects
Heat		
Sand		
No shadow		
No people		

2   Write a story in which a guilty person is escaping through a desert. Concentrate on how the character feels about what he or she has done and how the environment seems to reflect this through personification.

5 Describing things: the weather

A

Northeast England

It will be a fine and mostly dry day with sunny periods, a light southerly wind and a maximum temperature of 14°C. Tonight it will be clear at first, but increasing cloud will give patchy rain in places towards the end of the night. There will be a light southerly wind and a minimum temperature of 7°C.

Scotland

It will be a dry, bright, sunny day for many areas, with a few showers in the northwest. By mid-afternoon the wind will pick up, becoming quite strong with local gales in the northwest, where the showers will become more frequent and heavier, with thunderstorms. Other areas will stay mainly dry. The maximum temperature will be 16°C. During the night there will be showery rain in the northwest, extending eastwards to affect other western and northern areas by the morning. Winds will be strong, with early gales in the northwest.

Elsewhere it will be mainly dry but thicker cloud may spread to the extreme east by morning. The minimum temperature will be 6°C.

Southeast England

Early fog will clear, leaving a mainly dry day, with a maximum temperature of 15°C. There will be some sunshine, especially in the east, and a light southerly breeze, becoming cloudy during the night with heavy rain breaking out by morning. In the morning there will be a light northerly wind and a minimum temperature of 7°C.

Northwest England

After a dull and misty start it will brighten a little during the afternoon, with a maximum temperature of 14°C, but few places will see sunshine. There will be a light southerly breeze during the day, with variable wind direction during the night, when the mist will thicken to patchy fog. The minimum temperature will be 8°C.

B Key to weather icons

Sunny	Showers	Fair day	Part cloudy day	Drizzle	Cloudy	Part cloudy night	Rain

Forecast for Aberdeen

Time	Day	Outlook	Temperature	Wind direction	Speed
○	Mon		MAX: 13C/55F	SE	2 Kt
☽	Mon		MIN: 7C/45F	NW	12 Kt
○	Tue		MAX: 13C/55F	WSW	9 Kt
☽	Tue		MIN: 7C/45F	SSE	23 Kt
○	Wed		MAX: 11C/52F	SSW	15 Kt
☽	Wed		MIN: 7C/45F	SSW	20 Kt
○	Thur		MAX: 8C/46F	SSW	20 Kt
☽	Thur		MIN: 6C/43F	S	19 Kt

Forecast for Cardiff

Time	Day	Outlook	Temperature	Wind direction	Speed
○	Mon		MAX: 14C/57F	SW	6 Kt
☽	Mon		MIN: 6C/43F	WNW	9 Kt
○	Tue		MAX: 12C/54F	SSW	9 Kt
☽	Tue		MIN: 12C/54F	SSW	14 Kt
○	Wed		MAX: 14C/57F	WSW	7 Kt
☽	Wed		MIN: 7C/45F	WSW	16 Kt
○	Thur		MAX: 9C/48F	SSW	16 Kt
☽	Thur		MIN: 7C/45F	SW	10 Kt

Forecast for London

Time	Day	Outlook	Temperature	Wind direction	Speed
○	Mon		MAX: 16C/61F	WNW	10 Kt
☽	Mon		MIN: 10C/50F	W	9 Kt
○	Tue		MAX: 14C/57F	SW	6 Kt
☽	Tue		MIN: 10C/50F	S	15 Kt
○	Wed		MAX: 18C/64F	WSW	6 Kt
☽	Wed		MIN: 7C/45F	WSW	13 Kt
○	Thur		MAX: 11C/52F	SSW	12 Kt
☽	Thur		MIN: 7C/45F	SSW	13 Kt

Forecast for Newcastle

Time	Day	Outlook	Temperature	Wind direction	Speed
○	Mon		MAX: 13C/55F	NNW	4 Kt
☽	Mon		MIN: 8C/46F	W	10 Kt
○	Tue		MAX: 13C/55F	WSW	8 Kt
☽	Tue		MIN: 7C/45F	SSE	19 Kt
○	Wed		MAX: 13C/55F	SW	11 Kt
☽	Wed		MIN: 6C/43F	SW	18 Kt
○	Thur		MAX: 8C/46F	SSW	16 Kt
☽	Thur		MIN: 6C/43F	S	16 Kt

http://www.teletext.co.uk/weather

Read on!

1   In what ways does the information text about the weather (A) differ from the fictional description of the weather in Unit 4? Copy and complete the chart:

	Information text	Fictional text
Personal or impersonal language		
First, second or third person		
Use of figurative language		
Comparisons or similes		
Technical language		
Tense		
Facts		
Ideas/imagination		

2   What is the purpose of the weather forecast texts?
3   What does the reader expect from them?
4   How are the headings helpful?
5   What types of specific information are given in the weather forecasts for all areas?
6   List the words which are frequently used in the weather forecasts to describe: wind, rain, how clear the air is, cloud and temperature.

Give examples from the text.

Write on!

1   a) Read the charts (B) which give data from weather stations.
    b) Read the key.
    c) Look up any words you do not understand.
    d) List the words you will find useful in writing a four-day weather forecast for the cities shown on the charts:

Nouns	Verbs	Adjectives	Adverbs

2   Write a *general* four-day forecast for each city: Aberdeen, Cardiff, London and Newcastle.
    •   Your forecast should be a *general* description of the weather: precipitation, wind direction, wind speed, sunshine and temperature, without measurements (except for temperature).

Remember adverbs such as 'probably' which modify the verb 'to be' and adverbs which modify adjectives: 'mainly', 'mostly', 'fairly'.

Write in the style of the weather forecasts text (A).

Over to you!

1   Collect weather data for the area in which you live.
    •   Use data from your school weather station, local newspapers and the Internet.

2   Organise your data on a chart or database.
3   Write a weather report which will help your school to plan an outdoor event.

6 Describing processes

Television, the eyes and the brain

Television works by fooling our brains into believing they are seeing moving pictures. It does this by breaking down a picture into very small dots called pixels: the brain puts all the dots back together automatically. The television also breaks down a moving scene into separate pictures. When these pictures are put together in the right sequence and at the right speed, the brain converts them into a moving image, rather like when you draw a matchstick figure in different positions on the corners of the pages of a note book and flick through the note book: your brain sees the figure jumping, running or walking, depending on the pictures you have drawn and the order in which you have drawn them.

The image on a television screen is made up of tiny dots called pixels ▶

Pixels

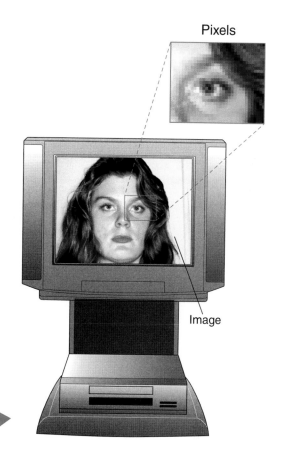

Image

▲ *A series of pictures drawn on the corners of pages can be made to 'move' when the pages are flicked.*

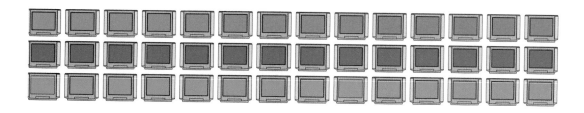

Describing processes

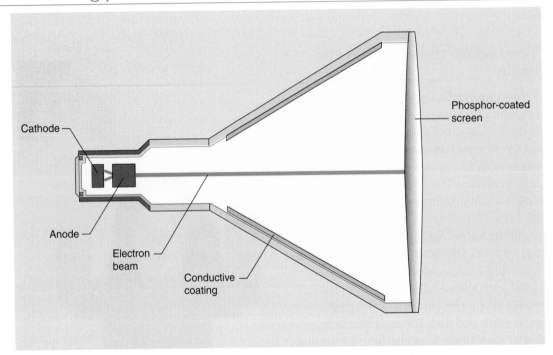

 Behind a television screen

The parts which create the picture

The main parts of a television set are the cathode-ray tube (CRT) and the phosphor-coated screen. The cathode is an electronic filament in a vacuum. A stream of electrons pours from the cathode via the anode into the vacuum. The anode accelerates the electrons and focuses them on to the phosphor-coated screen. As each electron hits the screen it lights up. This creates a picture. To make the picture appear to move, the beam of electrons sweeps quickly across the phosphor-coated screen in lines. As it does so it lights up pixels one after the other, creating parts of an image; the eye sees this as movement.

From broadcaster to television set

The television broadcaster sends out a video signal consisting of a stream of electrons. The signal carries information about how the pixels are to be lit up, including how the beam will sweep across the screen

Glossary

anode the electrode (conductor) through which a positive current enters the vacuum
cathode the electrode (conductor) through which a negative current enters the vacuum
cathode-ray tube a vacuum tube in which a controllable beam of electrons is focused on to a surface

electron a particle with a negative electrical charge which can travel through different materials and through a vacuum
filament a thin wire of high resistance
phosphor one of a range of substances which emit light
pixel the smallest element of the display on a computer monitor or television screen

Read on!

1 Which special abilities of the brain enable us to make sense of:
   - still pictures on a screen?
   - moving pictures on a screen?
2 From where do the electrons in the cathode-ray tube come?
3 After the stream of electrons pours from the cathode, what speeds it up?
4 What happens when an electron hits the phosphor-coated screen?
5 Of what is the picture on a television screen made up?

Write on!

1 Plan an explanation of how a television set works in a simple form so that a child aged about seven can understand it.
   - Make a note of the important ideas in the process: for example:

   > TV company sends out video message
   > video message = an invisible beam
   > television sets pick up the beam

   - Make a note of any parts of the text which require too high an understanding of electricity.
   - Make a note of which parts of the text to leave out and which parts will be useful.
   - Make a note of which parts can be simplified.

2 Use a flow chart to plan the explanation.
3 Write the explanation, using labelled diagrams where they will help.
4 Write a simple glossary.

Over to you!

1 Which features of the explanatory text about television sets help you to understand it?

2 Use these features and the Activity Sheet to help you to plan an explanatory text on a process about which you have learned at school: for example, something from science, technology or geography.

   Think about diagrams, drawings, headings, layout, and so on.

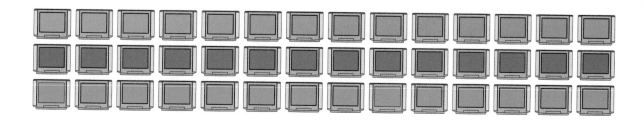

7 Making notes: mapping out ideas

Edward III came to the throne at the age of 14 and ruled England from 1327 to 1377. David II became King of Scotland at the age of 5, in 1329, and ruled until 1371.

A The reign of David II, son of Robert Bruce, was described by a contemporary as 'dark and drublie days'. David undid most of Bruce's good work and even offered to bequeath his kingdom to Edward III of England…

… In 1332 Edward III of England engineered a bid for the Scottish throne by John Balliol's son, Edward, who drove David II into exile and had himself crowned… it entailed the surrender of large parts of southern Scotland to English rule and, in 1341, Balliol was expelled and David reclaimed his throne.

But in 1346 David invaded England in support of his hard-pressed French allies and was defeated at Neville's Cross. For the next 11 years he remained a prisoner in England until released in 1357 on payment of a huge ransom. By 1363 the financial situation in Scotland had got so bad that David returned to London to negotiate a cancellation of the ransom payments if he bequeathed his throne to Edward III. The Scottish Parliament repudiated the proposal, preferring to bankrupt the country rather than surrender its independence.

from Kings and Queens: A Royal History of England and Scotland by Plantagenet Somerset Fry

B David II of Scotland … fled to France in 1334. He stayed there for seven years while the French court encouraged the Scots in rebellion in England. … The English beat the French at Crécy [in 1346], but Crécy was important for two other reasons. It cleared Edward's way to Calais and Calais became an English colony. Secondly, it proved that with the tactical use of longbow-men, mounted knights would no longer be the force they had been throughout the feudal era. And there's an aside. Edward III decreed that wool could only be exported through certain ports so that his officials could tax it. He needed the taxes to finance the war…

from This Sceptred Isle by Christopher Lee

C When Robert Bruce – King Robert I – died in 1329 he had achieved the apparently impossible: Scotland was a free and independent nation, its rights recognised by both England and the Pope … Scotland was strong and brimming with self-confidence, and its people looked forward to a long period of peace after the years of constant struggle and warfare.

No sooner was Bruce in his grave, however, than the legacy of his spectacular reign began to be undone. All the great loyalists who had supported him …would soon be dead. There was a child on the throne … the governance of Scotland would be in the hands of Guardians …

… In 1331 [Edward Balliol, the exiled son of John Balliol] was brought over to England from his family estates in Picardy. With Edward III's tacit compliance, he mounted a seaborne invasion of Scotland …

… The battle … ended in dreadful carnage … Scotland, it seemed, had fallen at the first blow. Edward Balliol … had himself crowned at Scone as King of Scots on 24 September 1332. The country now had two kings – the legitimate David II, and the usurper Edward Balliol … Two months later … Balliol swore homage and fealty to Edward III as lord superior of all Scotland.

from Scotland: The Story of a Nation by Magnus Magnusson

Glossary

compliance **agreement**
fealty **loyalty of a tenant to his lord**
Guardians **dukes and lords appointed to run the country while the king was a minor**

homage **a public declaration of allegiance to an overlord**
tacit **unspoken**

Read on!

1 From the passages, what impressions do you get of:
   a) David II of Scotland?
   b) Edward III of England?
   • Mention any different impressions you gain from the different texts.
   • Support your answers with quotations from the passages.

2 What do the passages tell you about alliances between England, Scotland and France?
3 What did the kings of England and Scotland do to try to gain power, money and lands?

Write on!

Make a note of any questions raised by the texts. Here are some examples:

> Why did Edward III want Edward Balliol, rather than David II, to be king of Scotland?

> Were any other countries involved in the struggle for power?

> What was happening in France?

Over to you!

1 Re-read the texts and make a note of the main events in the order in which they happened.
2 Use the Activity Sheet to make a time-line to show the events from the death of

Robert Bruce (1329) to the death of David II (1371).
3 Look for gaps in the time-line and make a note of any questions to which you would like to find the answer.

8 Point of view

In this story, Peter swaps bodies with the family cat and experiences what life is like from its point of view.

What a delight to walk on four soft white paws. He could see his whiskers springing out from the sides of his face, and he felt his tail curling behind him. His tread was light, and his fur was like the most comfortable of old woollen jumpers. As his pleasure in being a cat grew, his heart welled, and a tingling sensation deep in his throat became so strong that he could actually hear himself. Peter was purring. He was Peter Cat, and over there was William Boy …

That night Peter was too restless, too excited, too much of a cat to sleep.

Towards ten o'clock he slipped through the cat flap. The freezing night air could not penetrate his thick fur coat. He padded soundlessly towards the garden wall. It towered above him, but one effortless, graceful leap and he was up, surveying his territory. How wonderful to see into dark corners, to feel every vibration of the night air on his whiskers, and to make himself invisible, when at midnight a fox came up the garden path to root amongst the dustbins. All around he was aware of other cats, some local, some from far away, going about their night-time business, travelling their routes. After the fox, a young tabby had tried to enter the garden. Peter warned him off with a hiss and a flick of his tail. He had purred inwardly as the young fellow squealed in astonishment and took flight.

Not long after that, while patrolling the high wall that rose above the greenhouse, he came face to face with another cat, a more dangerous intruder. It was completely black, which was why Peter had not seen it sooner. It was the tom from next door, a vigorous fellow almost twice his size, with a thick neck and long powerful legs. Without even thinking, Peter arched his back and upended his fur to make himself look big.

'Hey puss,' he hissed, 'this is my wall and you're on it.'

The black cat looked surprised. It smiled. 'So it was your wall once, Grandad. What'ya going to do about it now?'

'Beat it, before I throw you off.' Peter was amazed at how strongly he felt. This was his wall, his garden, and it was his job to keep unfriendly cats out.

The black cat smiled again, coldly. 'Listen Grandad. It hasn't been your wall for a long time. I'm coming through. Out of my way or I'll rip your fur off.'

Peter stood his ground. 'Take another step, you walking flea circus, and I'll tie your whiskers around your neck.'

The black cat gave out a long laughing wail of contempt. But it did not take another step. All around, local cats were appearing out of the darkness to watch. Peter heard their voices.

A fight?

A fight!

The old boy must be crazy!

He's seventeen if he's a day.

The black cat arched its powerful spine and howled again, a terrible rising note.

Peter tried to keep his voice calm, but his words came out in a hiss. 'You don't take ssshort cutsss here without asking me firssst.'

The black cat blinked. The muscles in its fat neck rippled as it shrieked its laugh that was also a war cry.

On the opposite wall, a moan of excitement ran through the crowd which was still growing.

'Old Bill has flipped.'

'He's chosen the wrong cat to pick a fight with.'

'Listen, you toothless old sheep,' the black cat said through a hiss more penetrating than Peter's. 'I'm number one round here. Isn't that right?'

The black cat half turned to the crowd, which murmured its agreement. Peter thought the watching cats did not sound very enthusiastic.

'My advice to you,' the black cat went on, 'is to step aside. Or I'll spread your guts all over the lawn.'

Peter knew he had gone too far now to back down. He extended his claws to take a firm grip on the wall. 'You bloated rat! This is my wall d'you hear.'…

Peter had an old cat's body, but he had a young boy's mind. He ducked and felt the paw and its vicious outstretched claws go singing through the air above his ears. He had time to see how the black cat was supported momentarily on only three legs. Immediately he sprang forward, and with his two front paws pushed the tom hard in the chest. It was not the kind of thing a cat does in a fight and the number one cat was taken by surprise. With a yelp of astonishment, he slipped and tottered backwards, tipped off the wall and fell head first through the roof of the greenhouse below. The icy night air was shattered by the crash and musical tinkle of broken glass and the earthier clatter of breaking flowerpots. Then there was silence. The hushed crowd of cats peered

Point of view

about him was hurry and chaos. Kate could not find her satchel. The porridge was burned. Mr Fortune was in a bad mood because the coffee had run out and he needed three strong cups to start the day. The kitchen was a mess and the mess was covered in porridge smoke. And it was late late late!

Peter curled his tail around his back paws and tried not to purr too loudly. On the far side of the room was his old body with William Cat inside, and that body had to go to school. William Boy was looking confused. He had his coat on and he was ready to leave but he was wearing only one shoe. The other was nowhere to be found. 'Mum,' he kept bleating. 'Where's my shoe?' But Mrs Fortune was in the hallway arguing with someone on the phone.

Peter Cat half closed his eyes. After his victory he was desperately tired. Soon the family would be gone. The house would fall silent. When the radiator had cooled, he would wander upstairs and find the most comfortable of the beds. For old time's sake he would choose his own.

The day passed just as he had hoped. Dozing, lapping a saucer of milk, dozing again, munching through some tinned cat food that really was not as bad as it smelled – rather like shepherds pie without mashed potato. Then more dozing. Before he knew it, the sky outside was darkening and the children were home from school. William Boy looked worn out from a day of classroom and playground struggle. Boy-cat and cat-boy lay down together in front of the living-room fire. It was most odd, Peter Cat thought, to be stroked by a hand that only the day before had belonged to him.

down from their wall. They heard a movement, then a groan. Then, just visible in the gloom was the shape of the black cat hobbling across the lawn. They heard it muttering.

'It's not fair. Claws and teeth, yes. But pushing like that. It just isn't fair.'

'Next time,' Peter called down, 'you just ask permission.'

The black cat did not reply, but something about its retreating, limping shape made it clear it had understood.

The next morning Peter lay on the shelf above the radiator with his head cushioned on one paw, while the other dangled loosely in the rising warmth. All

from *The Daydreamer* by Ian McEwan

Read on!

This extract is written from the point of view of an animal. The use of accurate detail makes us really 'get into the animal's skin' and experience the world of a cat.

1 Copy and complete the chart with details from the passage:

What the cat sees	
What the cat hears	
What the cat feels	

2 Write out the stages in the cat-fight. Show how Peter wins the fight only because he uses human instincts and not cat ones.

3 What details of Peter in the house show his cat-like characteristics? How does he feel about this?

Write on!

1 Right from the start of the passage the author chooses verbs very carefully to give us the point of view of the cat. Copy and complete the chart to analyse the effect of the verbs in the first few paragraphs.

2 Continue with the adventures of the cat at night. Remember that you are writing from the point of view of the animal, so your actions and details must reflect the actions and responses of the animal. Use the Activity Sheet to help.

Verb used	Describing	Effect
springing	whiskers	This suggests a light, lively motion. The cat's whiskers are very sensitive and spring back into position.
curling		
slipped		
padded		
patrolling		

Over to you!

Choose another animal to 'get into the skin of'. Imagine that you are this animal for a few hours. What would the world be like?

Consider:

- the size of the animal in relation to the rest of the world
- what it would have to do to survive
- its daily routine
- special characteristics – how it would feed, walk, react with other members of the animal kingdom
- the language and images you will need to use to give your reader a sense of what the animal's life is like.

9 Narrators

The book from which these extracts are taken has two narrators and is told through their diaries. William G and Neaera H are two lonely people who decide to free some large turtles from London Zoo. In doing so, this changes their lives and their feelings about one another.

William G

… A lady came into the shop one afternoon, arty-intellectual type about my age or a little younger. She was wearing a long orange Indian-print skirt, an old velvet jacket, a denim shirt and expensive boots. Not at all bad looking. Rather troubled face, circles under the eyes. All at once I felt a strong urge to talk to her for a few hours about everything. And at the same time I felt an urge not to talk to her at all.

She drifted about the Natural History shelves for a time in a sleepwalking sort of way, picking up books and turning the pages without always looking at them. Then she picked up a book on sea turtles by Robert Bustard and read about a quarter of it where she stood. Eerie, the way she read, as if she'd simply forgotten to put the book down. And eerie she was, reading about sea turtles. Obviously I can't be the only one thinking about them but I had the shocking feeling that here was another one of me locked up alone in a brain with the same thoughts. Me, what's that after all? …

Neaera H

… George Fairbairn, the Head Keeper at the Aquarium, seemed quite willing to tell me anything I wanted to know about the turtles. I have the feeling that if I told him what's in my mind he might even help me do it and of course that frightens me.

I can't possibly do it alone. I'd need someone to handle the turtles in the van, I can't do any part of it really except pay the expenses. There'd be the long drive to Cornwall, it would be night time. I'd put them in the ocean at Polperro. The mystery of the turtles and their secret navigation is a magical reality, juice of life in a world gone dry. When I think of the turtles going into the ocean I think of it happening in that place that so badly needs new reality…

William G

… Saturday afternoon I went to the Zoo again. The sunlight was brilliant in Regent's Park, the air was sticky with ice-cream and soft drinks, people were rowing boats, there were girls in bikinis everywhere in the green grass and the young men walking with their shirts off. Inside the Aquarium it seemed darker than ever. I scarcely looked at the turtles, saw them out of the corner of my eye swooping like bad dreams in the golden-green.

I found George Fairbairn and we went into the room behind the turtle tank. There was another room off that one with a lot of small tanks in it, and he showed me a turtle somebody'd given the Aquarium when they found out how big it would grow. It was some kind of Ridley he thought but he wasn't sure which kind. I held it in my hand. One wouldn't expect a little black sea turtle to be cuddly but it was. It was about nine inches long, heavy and solid and wagged its flippers in a very docile way. It felt such a jolly nice piece of life.

After we'd been chatting for a while I came right out with it, standing there between two rows of tanks with a little turtle in my hand. There were big cockroaches hopping about on the floor.

'What if the turtle freak were to propose turtle theft to the Head keeper?' I said.

'Head keeper wouldn't be at all shocked by it,' he said.

'How would we go about it?' I said.

'Best time would be when we're cleaning and painting the tank,' he said. 'We take the turtles out and put them in the filters and they stay there for a week maybe while the maintaining gets done. So they're not on view and maybe for the whole week the Society wouldn't even know they're gone.' …

On my way to the South Gate I saw the woman who'd been in the shop asking about turtle books. She was coming towards me heading for the Aquarium I had no doubt …

Neaera H

… The man from the bookshop, would he be willing to drive the van? I think he's already thought about it, without me of course. Possibly it isn't something he'd like to share with anyone, I might be intruding. But the turtles are after all public, so to speak. Perhaps they no longer want the ocean and I'm wrong to impose my feelings on them. But I believe they do want the ocean, that must be in them. No, it's not always a comfort to find a like-minded person. If the bookshop man and I both have designs on the turtles we have got to muddle through it as decently as possible but there's little to be said between us beyond that …

from *Turtle Diary* by Russell Hoban

Read on!

1   Make a list of any features you notice about the diary form.

Details	What it tells me about their characters
William likes facts – notices detail	

2   The story deals with two different narrators. Copy and complete the chart to show how the author presents us with two very different characters.

3   What details used in *both* diaries ensure that we know we are dealing with one story?

4   How is the language of the two narrators different?

5   List the different concerns of both narrators about the planned turtle theft. What steps do they take to find out more?

6   What do you think this use of two narrators adds to the story? Would it have been better to have had one narrator telling you about characters and events?

Write on!

Complete the story of how William G and Neaera H rescue the turtles and set them free at Polperro. There is enough detail in the extract to help you. Use the chart:

*   Use the diary form and its style, as in the extract, to show the story from the point of view of two narrators.

*   Each of the diary extracts should contain the same basic information, but their interpretations of events may vary.
*   The extracts should also reflect the two different characters – how they think and feel.

Detail from the extract	
How I can use this in the story	
Tanks cleaned and turtles moved at this time	
Long drive to Cornwall in a hired van	

Over to you!

Narration through letter form is also an interesting way to achieve different perspectives on telling a story. Choose a well-known story of a disaster, for example the sinking of the *Titanic*, and tell your version of it through a series of letters written by different narrators. These could be:

*   yourself caught up in the disaster
*   a sailor who rescued you
*   a witness from another boat.

Remember to include enough common detail across all the narrators to ensure that your readers understand that they are reading about the same event. Use the Activity Sheet to help.

Think about what happened … but also how the characters reacted: what they said, what they did … what the feelings of the characters were … Think about the correct use of letter format.

10 Dialogue

In this extract from a novel, a group of children set off to find a mysterious street in the centre of the city.

Beyond the alley they came to a warren of grimy streets, where old women stood in the doorways, wearing sacks for aprons, and men in carpet slippers sat on the steps. Dogs nosed among crumpled paper in the gutter; a rusty bicycle wheel lay on the cobbles. A group of boys at the corner talked to a girl whose hair was rolled in brightly coloured plastic curlers.

'I don't like this, Nick,' said Helen. 'Should we go back up the alley?'

'No. They'll think we're scared. Look as though we know where we're going – taking a short cut; something like that.'

As the children walked past, all the eyes in the street watched them, without interest or hostility, but the children felt very uncomfortable, and walked close together. The girl on the corner laughed, but it could have been at something one of the boys said.

They went on through the streets.

'Perhaps it's not a good idea,' said Roland. 'Shall we go home?'

'Are you lost?' said Nicholas.

'No, but —'

'So what's all this?' said David.

Ahead of them the streets continued, but the houses were empty, and broken.

'That's queer,' said Nicholas. 'Come on: it looks as if Roland has something after all.'

'Let's go back,' said Roland.

'What, just when it's starting to be interesting? And isn't this the way to your Thursday Street?'

'Well – sort of – yes – I think so.'

'Come on, then.'

It was not one or two houses that were empty, but row after row and street after street. Grass grew in the cobbles everywhere, and in the cracks of the

pavement. Doors hung awry. Nearly all the windows were boarded up, or jagged with glass. Only at a few were there any curtains, and these twitched as the children approached. But they saw nobody.

'Isn't it spooky?' said David. 'You feel as if you ought to whisper. What if there was no one anywhere – even when we got back to Piccadilly?'

Helen looked through the window in one of the houses.

'This room's full of old dustbins!' she said.

Dialogue

'What's that chalked on the door?'
'Leave post at Number Four.'
'Number Four's empty, too.'
'I shouldn't like to be here at night, would you? said Helen.

'I keep feeling we're being watched,' said Roland.

'It's not surprising,' said David, 'with all these windows.'

'I've felt it ever since we were at the map at Piccadilly,' said Roland, 'and all the way up Oldham Road.'

'Oh, come off it, Roland,' said Nicholas. 'You're always imagining things.'

'Look there,' said David. 'They've started to bash the houses down. I wonder if we'll see a demolition gang working. They do it with a big iron ball, you know. They swing it from a crane.'

Something had certainly hit the street they were in now, for only the fronts of the houses were standing, and the sky showed on the inside of windows, and staircases led up a patchwork gable end of wallpaper.

At the bottom of the row the children stopped. The streets continued, with cobbles and pavements and lamp posts – but there were no houses, just fields of rubble.

'Where's your Thursday Street now?' said Nicholas.

'There,' said David.

He pointed to a salvaged nameplate that was balanced on a brickheap. 'Thursday Street.'

'You brought us straight here, anyway, Roland,' said Nicholas. 'The whole place has been flattened. It makes you think, doesn't it?'

'There's a demolition gang!' said Helen.

Alone and black in the middle of the wasteland stood a church. It was a plain Victorian building, with buttresses and lancet windows, a steep roof, but no spire. And beside it were a mechanical excavator and a lorry.

'I can't see anybody,' said Richard.

'They'll be inside,' said Nicholas. 'Let's go and ask if we can watch.'

from 'Thursday's Child' in *Elidor* by Alan Garner

Read on!

1. List the features of direct speech as shown in this dialogue, for example: the use and position of speech marks, the use of a new line for a new speaker.
2. Compare this dialogue with the speech in Unit 1. How are they different and why do you think the authors chose to write their dialogues in different ways?
3. How many characters are represented in this dialogue?
4. Sometimes their names are not used. How can you tell who is speaking?
5. When you use dialogue, you are not simply recording the words someone is speaking. You are also telling your reader about characters. Copy and complete the chart to show what you have learned about the characters:

Name of character	What he or she says	What I think it proves about his or her character

Write on!

Continue the dialogue, following the style and structure of the extract.

- Punctuate and set out the dialogue correctly.
- Continue to create a sense of the place through which they are walking.

- Copy and use this chart to help you plan:

What they say	How they say it
What it shows about their characters	How it moves forward the action or story

Over to you!

1. The author tends to use the verb 'said' to introduce the speech of most characters. Rewrite five pieces of the dialogue, changing the verb to something you feel may be more appropriate, for example: *'Perhaps it's not a good idea,'* **said** *Roland* (whispered, suggested, hinted, stated). A thesaurus may be useful for this activity.
2. Write a few sentences after each example to show how the meaning may have been changed by changing the verb.
3. Use adverbs after these new verbs to define your meaning more precisely, for example, *'Perhaps it's not a good idea,'* **whispered** *Roland,* **nervously**. This tells us a great deal more about his character and how he felt.
4. Imagine yourself and three friends returning from a disco late at night and walking through a very frightening area. Write the dialogue to show how you acted and how you felt. Make use of the techniques you have learned in this section. Use the Activity Sheet to help.

Names of characters	Weather conditions	Details of place

11 Autobiography

In this extract, Roald Dahl writes and reflects about an incident from his childhood.

At the age of eight, in 1924, I was sent away to boarding school in a town called Weston-super-Mare, on the south-west coast of England. Those were the days of horror, of fierce discipline, of no talking in the dormitories, no running in the corridors, no untidiness of any sort, no this or that or the other, just rules, rules and still more rules that had to be obeyed.

And the fear of the dreaded cane hung over us like the fear of death all the time.

'The headmaster wants to see you in his study.' Words of doom. They sent shivers over the skin of your stomach. But off you went, aged perhaps nine years old, down the long bleak corridors and through an archway that took you into the headmaster's private area where only horrible things happened and the smell of pipe tobacco hung in the air like incense. You stood outside the awful black door, not daring even to knock. You took deep breaths. If only your mother were here, you told yourself, she would not let this happen. She wasn't there. You were alone. You lifted a hand and knocked softly, once.

'Come in! Ah, yes, it's Dahl. Well Dahl, it's been reported to me that you were talking during prep last night.'

'Please sir, I broke my nib and I was only asking Jenkins if he had another one to lend me.'

'I will not tolerate talking in prep. You know that very well.'

Already this giant of a man was crossing to the tall corner cupboard and reaching up to the top of it where he kept his canes.

'Boys who break rules have to be punished.'

'Sir … I … I had a bust nib … I …'

'That's no excuse. I am going to teach you that it does not pay to talk during prep.'

He took down a cane that was about three feet long with a little curved handle at one end. It was thin and white and very whippy. 'Bend over and touch your toes. Over there by the window.'

'But sir…'

'Don't argue with me, boy. Do as you are told.'

I bent over. Then I waited. He always kept you waiting for about ten seconds, and that was when your knees began to shake.

'Bend lower, boy! Touch your toes!'

I stared at the toecaps of my black shoes and I told myself that any moment now this man was going to bash the cane so hard that the whole of my bottom would change colour. The welts were always very long, stretching right across both buttocks, blue black with brilliant scarlet edges, and when you ran your fingers over them ever so gently afterwards you could feel the corrugations.

Swish! … Crack!

Then came the pain. It was unbelievable, unbearable, excruciating. It was as though someone had laid a white-hot poker across your backside and pressed hard.

The second stroke would be coming soon and it was as much as you could do to stop putting your hands in the way to ward it off. It was the instinctive reaction. But if you did that, it would break your fingers.

Swish! … Crack!

The second one landed right alongside the first and the white-hot poker was pressing deeper and deeper into the skin.

Swish! … Crack!

The third stroke was where the pain always reached its peak. It could go no further. There was no way it could get worse. Any more strokes after that simply prolonged the agony. You tried not to cry out. Sometimes you couldn't help it. But whether you were able to remain silent or not, it was impossible to stop the tears. They poured down your cheeks in streams and dripped on the carpet.

The important thing was never to flinch upward or straighten up when you

were hit. If you did that, you got an extra one.

Slowly, deliberately, taking plenty of time, the headmaster delivered three more strokes, making six in all.

'You may go.' The voice came from a cavern miles away, and you straightened up slowly, agonisingly, and grabbed hold of your burning buttocks with both hands and held them as tight as you could and hopped out of the room on the very tips of your toes.

The cruel cane ruled our lives. We were caned for talking in the dormitory after lights out, for talking in class, for bad work, for carving our initials on the desk, for climbing over walls, for slovenly appearance, for flicking paper-clips, for forgetting to change into house-shoes in the evenings, for not hanging up our games clothes and above all for giving the slightest offence to any master. (They weren't called teachers in those days.) In other words, we were caned for doing everything that it was natural for small boys to do.

from Boy by Roald Dahl

Read on!

1 Which pronoun does the author use about himself throughout the extract?

2 In the first paragraph, what feeling does the author show about his childhood days?

3 Does the description of the episode prove him right?

4 What detail makes you feel sorry for the child as he stands outside the headteacher's door?

5 Why do you think the boy describes the caning in such minute detail? Copy the chart and note how he uses all his senses:

Event	Detail	Senses used
The first stroke		
The second stroke		
The third stroke		

Write on!

1 Consider how Roald Dahl uses detail to make his writing very immediate. Copy the chart and find examples from the extract. Then complete the Activity Sheet.

Speech of a child from the 1920s	
Speech of an adult from the 1920s	
How a frightened child would think	
How a frightened child would behave	
Details to show how painful it was	
Sound effects	

2 Continue writing the next episode in Roald Dahl's school life in the 1920s or write about an unhappy incident at school from your own experience.

- Whichever option you choose will only be successful if you select details and events and write about characters' reactions which are true to their time. For example, in the 1920s there was no television, and phones were rare.
- School was very different from now. You may have to do some research.

Over to you!

Write an excerpt from your own autobiography.

Decide:

- Which part of your life story will be of most interest to others? What are the most important events in your life so far?
- How will you start this in an interesting way?
- What details will make the story come alive for others?

Remember:

- Use the 'I' form – the first person. This is you writing about *you*!
- Avoid writing about all the details you can think of. Cut them down to the most important or the most interesting.
- It can become boring to work through your life story, event by event. You can fill in 'the gaps' if you think it is necessary.

It can often be interesting when you do not start at the beginning of an event. Use the flashback technique.

12 Making notes: planning a biography

A

Bell, Alexander Graham 1847–1922
US inventor

Alexander Graham Bell was born in Edinburgh, Scotland, the son of Alexander Melville Bell. Educated there and in London, he first worked as an assistant to his father in teaching elocution (1868–70). In 1872 he opened a school in Boston for training teachers of the deaf, and in 1873 he was appointed Professor of Vocal Physiology at Boston, where he devoted himself to the teaching of deaf-mutes and to spreading his father's system of 'visible speech'.

After experimenting with various acoustical devices he produced the first intelligible telephonic transmission with a message to his assistant on 5 June 1875. He patented the telephone in 1876, defended the patent against Elisha Gray, and formed the Bell Telephone Company in 1877. In 1880 he established the

Volta Laboratory, and invented the photophone (1880) and the graphophone (1887). He also founded the journal Science (1883). After 1897 his principle interest was in aeronautics.

from
Chambers Biographical Dictionary,
1997

B The young man [*Alexander Graham Bell – Aleck*] received his primary education at home from his mother, and at an early age showed an inventive spirit. After hearing his father remark one day that his watch needed cleaning, Aleck dutifully took the timepiece apart and cleaned it – using a brush, a cake of soap, and a bowl of water. He later recalled that his father was 'not enthusiastic over the results of my industry.'

The father of one of Aleck's friends, Ben Herdman, was happier with the fruits of the boys' creativity. Mr Herdman owned a flour mill, where the two boys were constantly getting into mischief. Finally the exasperated miller called them into his office and, after speaking rather sternly to them, demanded, 'Now boys, why don't you do something useful?'

'What shall we do?' asked Aleck offhandedly.

Mr Herdman thrust his arm into a bag of grain and said, 'If only you could take the husks off this wheat you would be doing something useful indeed.'

Apparently Mr Herdman and his workman hadn't been able to find a way to separate the husks from the grains easily.

First the two boys found they could remove the husks with a little nail brush, although 'it involved a good deal of hard work…,' Aleck later claimed. Then they decided they needed something more elaborate to do the same thing on a larger scale. Aleck thought he had the perfect solution: an old vat with a rotating paddle wheel inside, which the boys had found on their explorations of the mill. The walls of the vat were 'provided with brushes of something rough'. The boys poured the grain into the machine, and the rotation of the wheel forced the grain against the rough surface, effectively removing the husks…

Half a century later, Aleck recalled that 'it was a proud day for us when we boys marched into Mr Herdman's office, presented him with our sample of cleaned wheat, and suggested paddling the wheat' in the old vat. Aleck believed that the machine was still in use at the mill fifty years later, and commented that 'Herdman's injunction to do something useful was my first incentive to invention, and the method of cleaning wheat was the first fruit of my efforts.'

In those early days Aleck showed real

Making notes: planning a biography

musical ability. He could play by ear and improvise at the piano at a very early age, and he received an extensive musical education from the famous pianist Auguste Benoit Bertini. 'My dream as a young man was to become a musician,' he told an interviewer later…

The year 1860 was a turning point for Aleck, when he went to London to spend a year with his grandfather. Alexander Bell gave the thirteen-year-old boy lessons in elocution, reading Shakespeare and the treatment of speech defects …

… When Aleck's father came to London the following year, they went together to see the famous scientist Sir Charles Wheatstone, who was said to have a machine that could pronounce human words. Often such 'speaking automatons', exhibited as wonders at fairs and museums, were just ventriloquists' dummies … 'I saw Sir Charles manipulate the machine and heard it speak,' Bell later wrote, 'and although the articulation was disappointingly crude, it made a great impression upon my mind.'

Later, back in Edinburgh, Mr Bell challenged his sons to construct a machine to recreate human speech more accurately. 'My brother Melville and I attacked the problem together, and divided up the work,' Bell remembered. 'He undertook to make the lungs and throat of the apparatus while I made the tongue and mouth.'

It was not an easy task. The boys made several different versions of a larynx of tin and rubber and blew through it to make sounds. Using a human skull as a model, Aleck constructed a jaw, upper gum, hard palate, teeth and other parts from gutta-percha which resembles hard rubber …

… After they had connected the pieces and experimented with it, the boys were ready for the big test. They took the machine out … and 'made it yell.' Bell later wrote that it really sounded like a baby in great distress. 'Mamma, Mamma' came forth with heart-rending effect. We heard someone say, 'Good gracious, what can be the matter with that baby', and then footsteps were heard. This, of course, was just what we wanted. We slipped quietly into our house, and closed the door …Our triumph and happiness were complete' …

Aleck had a natural sympathy for the deaf, since his mother, Eliza Symonds Bell, had lost much of her hearing…As Aleck played the family piano, Eliza would sit with her hearing tube pressed against the wood of its sounding board…

…Aleck performed an entertaining bit of speech therapy: he taught the family's Skye terrier to 'speak'. Although, of course, the dog lacked the essential physical apparatus to create human sounds, Aleck first trained him to growl, using pieces of meat as an inducement. The little terrier 'soon became delighted to growl for food,' Aleck recalled later. 'He would sit up on his hind legs, and growl continuously until I motioned him to stop. Then he was rewarded with a morsel of food.'

Going a little further, Aleck took the dog's mouth in his hands, opening and closing the animal's lips while he growled. 'Ma ma ma ma,' the dog would utter.

Aleck then placed his thumb under the dog's lower jaw, between the bones, and caused him to say, 'Ga ga ga ga.' It was not long before he could be made to utter 'Ga ma ma.' After learning to move the dog's mouth in other ways, Aleck could make him pronounce the syllables 'ow', 'ah' and 'oo'.

'The fame of the dog spread,' Bell recalled. 'Many were the visitors who came to the house to see this dog sit up on his hind legs and, with a little assistance from my hand, growl forth the words 'How are you grandmamma?' The dog appeared to enjoy the applause and afterward would sit up and growl again, trying to do the performance alone …

from *Alexander Graham Bell*
by Edwin S. Grosvenor and Morgan Wesson

Read on!

1. In which person are texts A and B written? (Notice the pronouns used to refer to Alexander Graham Bell.) Give examples from the texts to support your answer.
2. What sort of tone does each text have: for example, factual, expressive, explaining, evoking feelings.
3. The biography (B) includes words written or spoken by Alexander Graham Bell although it was written after he died. Change these to indirect speech (for example, 'Bell said that …', or 'Bell exclaimed …').

Compare your versions with the original. Can you see why the authors did not write in this way?

4. In what ways does this differ from the autobiographical accounts in Units 2 and 11? Your answers to questions 1 to 3 will help you to answer this.
5. What does the biography tell you about the factors which led to Alexander Graham Bell's interest in the telephone?
6. What special talents or skills helped Bell to invent the telephone?

Write on!

1. List the dates and events in the biographical dictionary (A) which do not appear in the extract from the biography (B).
2. Read a biography of someone about whom you have learned in history and list any events and dates which you think should be included in an entry for a biographical dictionary.
3. Write a brief entry on this person for a biographical dictionary.

4. Your entry should be 100 words long. Check its length. If it is too short, look through your notes to find anything important which you can add; if it is too long, find ways to shorten it. Can anything be deleted or shortened? Is there a shorter way in which to write other parts?

When counting words for the biographical dictionary entry, between 90 and 110 words are acceptable.

Over to you!

Plan a biography of someone you know:

1. List the important information (see the Activity Sheet).
2. Make a note of anything the person has achieved at school, at work, at home or in leisure activities.
3. Ask the person to describe any memories he or she has of significant events in his or her life (events which have influenced things he or she did later). Tape record or write what he or she says.
4. Plan the biography. It should include:
   - an introduction to say what is important about the person: his or her special qualities or achievements
   - chapters into which the main sections of the person's life are described
   - an ending which sums up the person's life so far.

13 Explanations

Writing in Ancient Egypt

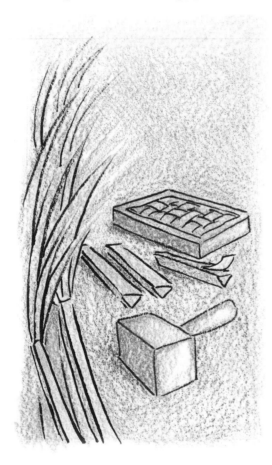

pulp is cut into thin strips forty centimetres long. After this the strips are laid in the same direction and a second layer is placed on top at right angles to it. The layers are then pounded together with a wooden mallet and dried in the sun to produce an acceptable surface for writing. Before use, the papyrus sheets are cut to the appropriate size with special knives and the surface smoothed with a piece of stone. Since papyrus is so time-consuming to make, writing was practised on wooden boards which could be wiped clean, limestone flakes and pottery pieces.

On papyrus, the Ancient Egyptians wrote mainly from right to left. However, because hieroglyphs often had to fit into confined or awkward spaces, a scribe had to be able to write from left to right and up and down as well!

The Ancient Egyptians developed a system of writing based on pictures, more than 700 in all, called 'hieroglyphs'. This word is derived from Greek: *hieros* meaning 'sacred' and *gluphe* meaning 'carving'. Hieroglyphs were used for more than 3,000 years.

Much of the language is written on papyrus using reed pens and black ink made by scraping carbon from fire-blackened vessels and mixing it with gum and water. Headings are often written in red made from ochre.

Papyrus is made from the *Cyperus papyrus*, a plant which grows along the banks of the Nile. First, the outer rind of the papyrus is removed. Then the inner

Read on!

1   The purpose of an explanation is to explain how things are done or how things work. Explain how you can tell that this extract is an explanation.
2   On what explanation does the passage really focus?
3   Where does this occur in the passage?
4   What do the first two paragraphs aim to do?
5   Why is it important for explanations to have an order?
6   Which is the main tense used?
7   What do you notice about the kinds of words used to connect the various sentences in this explanation?
8   Copy and complete the chart to show how explanations can be used in many subjects:

Subject	Example of explanation
History	
Geography	
Science	
Music	

Write on!

1   Make notes from the passage about the process of making papyrus. Use a chart like this one to help.

Stages	What happened
1	Made from plants grown along river Nile

2   Write a piece for a history book in your own words about papyrus, using these subheadings:
    *   Origin
    *   Purpose
    *   Process involved
    *   Any disadvantages.

Over to you!

1   Use the Activity Sheet to help in this activity. Explanations focus on **how** things work or **why** things happen. Choose one of the explanations from another subject – as discussed in the first section – either a **how** or **why** explanation.
    *   Follow the various stages in writing your explanation.
    *   Use the notes on your Activity Sheet to write the explanation.
    *   Provide any necessary diagrams to make the process easier to understand.

2   Write another explanation – one of the other kinds not dealt with in question 1.

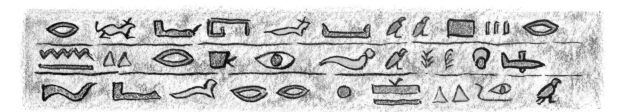

14   Newspaper reports

A

Highway panic as snake legs it to freedom

Esther Addley

A family outing to a pet shop to buy dog shampoo ended with a police armed response unit prowling the A46 in Warwickshire, after a three foot snake slithered out of a bag of shopping and up a car passenger's trouser leg.

David Wilson, 29, of Warwick, was travelling home from Coventry on Monday with his wife and two young children when the snake emerged from a carrier bag.

The intruder was, in fact, a non-poisonous corn snake.

Mr Wilson said yesterday: 'I saw a snake coming out of the bag and it started climbing up my leg.

'I just panicked. I was hysterical. My wife saw the snake's head and it set her off, and then my daughter started crying.'

Mr Wilson's wife, Natalie, who was driving, managed to pull over. The couple fled the vehicle with their two children, aged six and eighteen months.

By chance, a police armed response unit was travelling down the dual carriageway near Leek Wootton, and gave assistance.

'One of the officers joked that if the worst came to the worst, he could always shoot the snake,' said Mr Wilson, a supermarket manager.

Mrs Wilson had gone to the pet shop to buy dog shampoo, while her husband had a haircut. While she was in the shop, she also bought a fish tank suction pipe, and it is thought that the snake must have earlier taken up its abode inside the pipe.

The reddish-brown reptile, also known as the red rat-snake, is native to the south-eastern United States, where its natural habitat is in abandoned buildings and rubbish piles. It lives on rodents and small birds.

The stowaway was eventually recovered from the car's engine and taken to a nearby pet shop for safety.

Mr Wilson added: 'it may have been only about three feet long but as far as I was concerned it was ten feet and a python.'

from *The Guardian*, 18 October 2000

B

- Wood Farmhouse in Wetford was built in the sixteenth century.
- Roman and Saxon remains were found there earlier this year.
- James Smith inherited the farmhouse when his father died.
- He used to run another farm in the nearby village of Drybridge.
- He closed this farm.
- He applied for planning permission to demolish Wood Farmhouse and to build sixteen houses on the site.
- These houses would sell for a total of about £4 million.
- Wood Farmhouse was valued at £300,000.

- Wetford villagers were very concerned when they heard that the 450-year-old building was to be pulled down: it was part of the village heritage.
- The villagers contacted Wishmoor council.
- Inspectors from English Heritage arranged to inspect Wood Farmhouse on Monday to decide if it should be designated as a listed building.
- On Sunday, James Smith took out an old fireplace at Wood Farmhouse.
- By Monday morning Wood Farmhouse had completely collapsed. All that remained was a pile of rubble.
- No furniture could be seen in the rubble.

Read on!

1 Headlines are important: they make the reader decide whether or not to read the article. How does this headline (A) appeal to the reader?

Think about humour.

- What questions does the headline make you ask?
  For example: Where did it happen?
- Does the article answer these questions? What are the answers?

2 What information does the report give about the people involved and the snake? Copy and complete the chart as you find each piece of information.

Mr Wilson	His family	The snake

3 To engage the reader's interest the reporter begins by setting the scene: she does not present the events in the exact order in which they happened, but organises the information into paragraphs with interesting openings. List the main events in the order in which they happened.

4 The reporter recreates the feelings of the people involved in the incident by her choice of words. List the words which create a feeling or atmosphere and say what feeling or atmosphere:

Example: panic (as it says – panic), prowling (searching, like an animal in the wild).

Write on!

1 Read the information in B, which has been extracted from a news story, and arrange it in the order in which you would write it for a newspaper article.
2 Imagine the reactions of people living in Wetford village, the response of the local parish council, the local authority and heritage organisations. Imagine what they and James Smith might have said to newspaper reporters.

With your group, enact the interviews while one or two members of the group take notes (or make a tape recording).

Over to you!

Use the above information and your group's notes or recording of the enacted interviews to plan a newspaper report on the demolition of Wood Farmhouse.

Think of an eye-catching headline and an interesting opening paragraph.

Think about why the newspaper is covering this story.

15 Reference texts: the Internet

Someone who wanted to find out about the Domesday Book entered the key phrase 'Domesday Book' on an Internet search engine. One of the websites which she thought would be useful was http://domesdaybook.co.uk/.

A

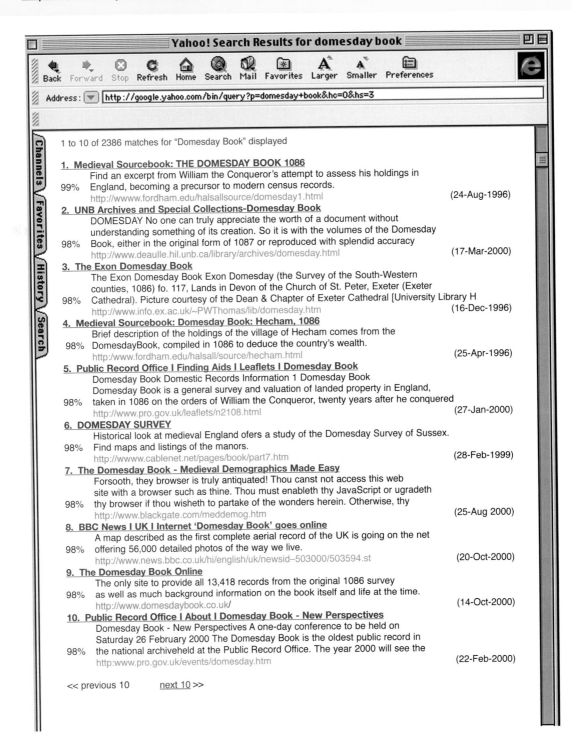

Yahoo! Search Results for domesday book

Address: http://google.yahoo.com/bin/query?p=domesday+book&hc=0&hs=3

1 to 10 of 2386 matches for "Domesday Book" displayed

1. Medieval Sourcebook: THE DOMESDAY BOOK 1086
Find an excerpt from William the Conqueror's attempt to assess his holdings in
99% England, becoming a precursor to modern census records.
http://www.fordham.edu/halsallsource/domesday1.html   (24-Aug-1996)

2. UNB Archives and Special Collections-Domesday Book
DOMESDAY No one can truly appreciate the worth of a document without
understanding something of its creation. So it is with the volumes of the Domesday
98% Book, either in the original form of 1087 or reproduced with splendid accuracy
http://www.deaulle.hil.unb.ca/library/archives/domesday.html   (17-Mar-2000)

3. The Exon Domesday Book
The Exon Domesday Book Exon Domesday (the Survey of the South-Western
counties, 1086) fo. 117, Lands in Devon of the Church of St. Peter, Exeter (Exeter
98% Cathedral). Picture courtesy of the Dean & Chapter of Exeter Cathedral [University Library H
http://www.info.ex.ac.uk/~PWThomas/lib/domesday.htm   (16-Dec-1996)

4. Medieval Sourcebook: Domesday Book: Hecham, 1086
Brief description of the holdings of the village of Hecham comes from the
98% DomesdayBook, compiled in 1086 to deduce the country's wealth.
http://www.fordham.edu/halsall/source/hecham.html   (25-Apr-1996)

5. Public Record Office I Finding Aids I Leaflets I Domesday Book
Domesday Book Domestic Records Information 1 Domesday Book
Domesday Book is a general survey and valuation of landed property in England,
98% taken in 1086 on the orders of William the Conqueror, twenty years after he conquered
http://www.pro.gov.uk/leaflets/n2108.html   (27-Jan-2000)

6. DOMESDAY SURVEY
Historical look at medieval England ofers a study of the Domesday Survey of Sussex.
98% Find maps and listings of the manors.
http://wwww.cablenet.net/pages/book/part7.htm   (28-Feb-1999)

7. The Domesday Book - Medieval Demographics Made Easy
Forsooth, they browser is truly antiquated! Thou canst not access this web
site with a browser such as thine. Thou must enableth thy JavaScript or ugradeth
98% thy browser if thou wisheth to partake of the wonders herein. Otherwise, thy
http://www.blackgate.com/meddemog.htm   (25-Aug 2000)

8. BBC News I UK I Internet 'Domesday Book' goes online
A map described as the first complete aerial record of the UK is going on the net
98% offering 56,000 detailed photos of the way we live.
http://www.news.bbc.co.uk/hi/english/uk/newsid–503000/503594.st (20-Oct-2000)

9. The Domesday Book Online
The only site to provide all 13,418 records from the original 1086 survey
98% as well as much background information on the book itself and life at the time.
http://www.domesdaybook.co.uk/   (14-Oct-2000)

10. Public Record Office I About I Domesday Book - New Perspectives
Domesday Book - New Perspectives A one-day conference to be held on
Saturday 26 February 2000 The Domesday Book is the oldest public record in
98% the national archiveheld at the Public Record Office. The year 2000 will see the
http:www.pro.gov.uk/events/domesday.htm   (22-Feb-2000)

<< previous 10   next 10 >>

B

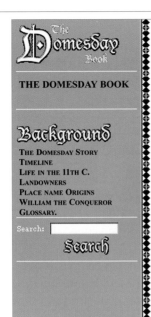

THE DOMESDAY BOOK

Background

THE DOMESDAY STORY
TIMELINE
LIFE IN THE 11TH C.
LANDOWNERS
PLACE NAME ORIGINS
WILLIAM THE CONQUEROR
GLOSSARY.

Search: [   ]

Search

The Domesday Book was commissioned in December 1085 by William the Conqueror, who invaded England in 1066. The first draft was completed in August 1086 and contained records for 13,418 settlements in the English counties south of the rivers Ribble and Tees (the border with Scotland at the time).

This site has been set up to enable visitors to find out the history of the local area as it was in the 11th century. The site does not yet contain all the information contained in the original text, however does include information for every settlement existing in 1086. If you would like the complete record for a certain place, please click on 'Contact us' and send your request.

C

Lancashire

Major entries

Heysham Land of the King in Yorkshire…In Halton Earl Tosti had 6c. of land taxable. In Alcliffe 2c., Thurnham 2c., Hillam 1c., Lancaster 6c., Kirk Lancaster 2c., Hutton 2c., Newton 2c., Overton 4c., Middleton 4c., Heaton 2c., HEYSHAM *HESSAM* 4c., Oxcliffe 2c., Poulton (le Sands) 2c., Torrisholme 2c., Skerton 6c., Bare 2c., Slyne 6c., Bolton (le Sands) 4c., Keller 6c., Stapleton Terne 2c., Newsham 2c., Carnforth 2c. All these villages belong to Halton.

Argarmeles Roger de Poitou held the undermentioned land. Between the Ribble and the Mersey. In (West) Derby Hundred [a list follows, naming 45 holdings, including:] Wigbert held ARGARMELES *ERENGERMELES*. 2 carucates of land. The value was 8s. This land was exempt apart from tax.

Warrington Roger de Poitou held the undermentioned land. Between the Ribble and the Mersey…In Warrington Hundred. King Edward held WARRINGTON *WALINTUNE* with 3 outliers. 1 hide. To the manor itself belonged 34 drengs and they had as many manors in which there were 34 carucates of land and 1 1/2 hides. St. Elfin's held 1 carucate of land exempt from all customary dues except tx. The whole manor with the Hundred paid £15 less 2s in revenue to the King. Now 2 ploughs in Lordship; 8 men with 1 plough. Thse men hold land there: Roger 1 carucate of land; Theobald 1 carucates; Warin 1 carucate; Ralp 5 carucates; William 2 hies and 4 carucates of land; Aethelhard 1 hide and 1/2 carucate; Osmund 1 carucate of land. Total value £4 10s; value of the lordship £3 10s.

Ribchester Land of the King in Yorkshire…Amounderness. In Preston, Earl Tosti, 6c. taxable. These lands belong there. Ashton 2c., Lea 1c., [a list of 59 towns follows, including RIBCHESTER *RIBELCASTRE* 2C.] All these villages and 3 churches belong to Preston. 16 of them have a few inhabitants, but how many is not known. The rest are waste. Roger de Poitou had them.

Read on!

1 Copy the chart and list the numbers of the websites listed in A which would help you to find out about the places recorded in the Domesday Book. Explain how the website might be useful:

Website no.	How it might be useful	Key words in the details given

Advantages of web page		Disadvantages of web page	
Advantage	Reason	Disadvantage	Reason

2 Was 'Domesday Book' the best key phrase to enter in the search engine? Explain why you think this. What other words or phrases could have been entered?

3 Read the web pages of The Domesday Book website (B and C). How does this differ from reading a book on the topic?

Copy the chart, list the differences and describe their advantages and disadvantages:

4 About which of the following does the Domesday Book website give information (and what, briefly, does it tell you):
a) who commissioned the Domesday Book?
b) when it was commissioned?
c) why it was commissioned?
d) whether your city, town or village was included in it?

The Activity Sheet helps you to evaluate sources of information (books and websites) about any topic you are studying.

Write on!

1 What information does the Domesday Book give about each settlement listed in it?

2 Look at the first page of the website (B). On which heading can you click to find the meanings of the words used in the entry on Lancashire?

3 Open the website on a computer and use it to find the meanings of the following words in the Lancashire entry: hide, caracute, dreng.

4 Find out from the website who the main landowner in Lancashire was.

Over to you!

Use the website to find out:

• what your city, town or village was like in 1086

• what were the main settlements in England at that time

• who were the important landowners.

16 Giving directions

The Liverpool Heritage Walk starts and finishes at Lime Street Station. It covers a distance of 11.5 kilometres and is marked by seventy-five numbered square metal Markers set into pavements. There are also City of Liverpool plaques in red, blue and green: red plaques mark sites associated with historical events and notable people; blue plaques mark buildings of architectural importance and green plaques mark the positions (or approximate positions) of demolished buildings. Text A is adapted from a section of the walk.

A

59 to 62: The centre of Victorian trade

On the corner of **Crosshall Street** and **Victoria Stree**t, Marker 59 and a green plaque indicate the position of the Beehive Public House, which was well-known in Victorian times for its rat pit where people used to place bets on the number of rats a dog would kill. Walk southwest along Victoria Street. On the left you will see the **Midland Railway Goods Office**, designed by **William Culshaw** and **Henry Sumners** and completed in 1874. In this building the despatch of goods by rail to and from other parts of the country was organised. On the carved spandrels (roughly triangular spaces between the tops of the arches) are the names of the towns served by the Midland Railway. The building is now the Conservation Centre of the Museums and Galleries of Merseyside and houses part of the Museum's collection of large exhibits.

The next street on your right is Sir Thomas Street, named after **Sir Thomas Johnson** (1670–1729), a tobacco merchant who was Liverpool's MP for 21 years.

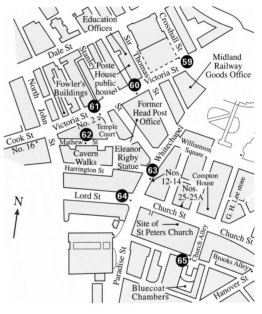

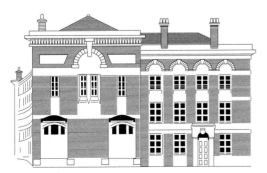

Midland Railway Goods Office

Continue along **Victoria Street** to the next street on the right where you will see Marker 60 on the corner of **Cumberland Street** (named after **William, Duke of Cumberland**, who was supported by the Liverpool Blues Regiment during the 1745 Jacobite Rebellion in Scotland). Continue along Victoria Street, past the former **Head Post Office** on your left.

Take the next left – **Stanley Street**; there, on the south-western wall of the former Head Post Office, opposite to the restaurant Casa Italia, sits **Eleanor Rigby**, the character created by the **Beatles** in their song. The story goes that **Paul McCartney** named her after the actress Eleanor Bron and the name on a shop which he saw in Bristol, but at St Peter's church in Woolton, a suburb of Liverpool, there is a grave marked 'Eleanor Rigby',

Giving directions

which suggests that she was a real person. Paul McCartney and John Lennon first met at St Peter's summer fair. Maybe they were inspired by the name on the grave.

The singer **Tommy Steele** made the bronze sculpture after he performed in the musical *Half a Sixpence* at the Liverpool Empire Theatre. He offered it to Liverpool City Council for three old pence (half a sixpence). Set inside the bronze are: a four-leaved clover (for nature and luck), a page of the Bible (for the spirit), a football sock (for leisure), two comics, the *Dandy* and the *Beano* (for humour), and four sonnets (for romance).

Retrace your steps along Stanley Street and turn left to continue walking southwest along **Victoria Street** (Marker 61). Victoria Street was built between 1867 and 1868 to cope with the increasing traffic in the city resulting from the rise in trade of the time. On the western side is the office block **No. 2 Temple Court** with its plaster façade – the only eighteenth-century building to survive the road-building scheme in Victoria Street and is still standing.

On the opposite side of Victoria Street

No. 16 Cook Street

are **Fowler's Buildings**, designed by **Sir James Picton**, completed in 1964. The Fowler family ran a fish-salting business when Liverpool was a busy port: fish were salted in the factory behind the building and the offices were at the front.

Continue southwest along Victoria Street until you come to **North John Street**, which crosses it. Go straight ahead into **Cook Street**, the continuation of Victoria Street, and look at **number 16** with its façade of three giant bays of a Venetian window filled in with plate-glass. When do you think it was built? It looks very modern but, in fact, it was built in 1866. Its style was very advanced for its time and the architect, **Peter Ellis**, was fiercely criticised.

adapted from *Liverpool Heritage Walk*
by Philip Browning and John Edwards, for Liverpool City Planning Department

---

B Cavern Walks shopping and office mall opened 1984 on site of Cavern Club (demolished to make way for underground railway). Designed by L'pool architect David Backhouse. On g. floor of atrium – sculpture of Beatles by John Doubleday. On the wall nr Mathew St entrance – terracotta sculpture by Cynthia Lennon (1st wife of John Lennon): roses and doves, symbolising peace. Opp C. Walks, on wall of office block in Mathew St – bronze sculpt by L'pool sculptor Arthur Dooley: 'Four Lads Who Shook the World'. Above arched opening of car park of C. Walks (Harrington St), engraved on keystone: gorilla putting on lipstick! (By Hathernware, terracotta manufacturers). Story: London architect visited C. Walks (dislikes decoration on buildings): 'Art is to architecture as lipstick is to a gorilla' – C. Walks architect wanted to record this.

12–14 Whitechapel (now Ann Somers shop) once NEMS (North End Music Stores) owned by Brian Epstein – got many requests for record My Bonnie recorded in W Germany by Beatles. Went to Cavern Club to hear them; became their manager.

'Holy Corner' (from names of streets wh. meet there: Whitechapel, Church Street and Paradise). Church St named after Church of St Peter (on southern side, now demolished). Gold Maltese cross set into stone step from the church, set into pavement outside Top Shop commemorates church.

25-25A Church St (now HMV store) site of 1st Woolworth's in Europe (1909). On wall above level of roof of next building: 'Woolworth's 3d and 6d Store'.

Compton House (now M&S) once Jeffrey's dept store (burned down 1865) became Compton House Hotel. Carved in stone on its corners: coats of arms: Royal Coat of Arms and coat of arms of USA (hotel popular with US visitors). Above the cornice: coat of arms of L'pool: Liver Bird (cormorant) with seaweed in mouth.

Bluecoat Chambers oldest building in city centre (1717), built as charity school. Now centre for arts, with restaurant and craft shops. Bluecoat school there until 1906.

Read on!

1 List the words used in the guide which tell you the directions in which to walk or to look.
2 List any features of the Heritage Walk which make it easy to follow and easy to relate the text to real things seen during the walk.
3 Is anything missing? List any questions you want to ask about things you would see on the route.
4 If you followed the walk, for what would you look out?
5 What do you learn during this walk about:
   • Liverpool's industrial and commercial past?
   • Liverpool's connections with the arts and entertainment?

Write on!

Look at the map and read the notes (B). Write a continuation in the style of the Heritage Walk Guide to take the reader from Marker number 61 to numbers 62, 63, 64 and 65.

Over to you!

1 Make notes about what visitors would see if they followed a heritage walk near where you live. List the buildings, statues, objects of historical or cultural importance, and sites of demolished buildings or other important features which you would include. The work could be shared with your group.
2 Make notes about sources of information, such as local tourist information offices, books, leaflets and websites.
3 Make notes about how you would plan and organise a guided walk. The Activity Sheet helps you to organise this plan.

17 Planning and sequencing

The Plumber

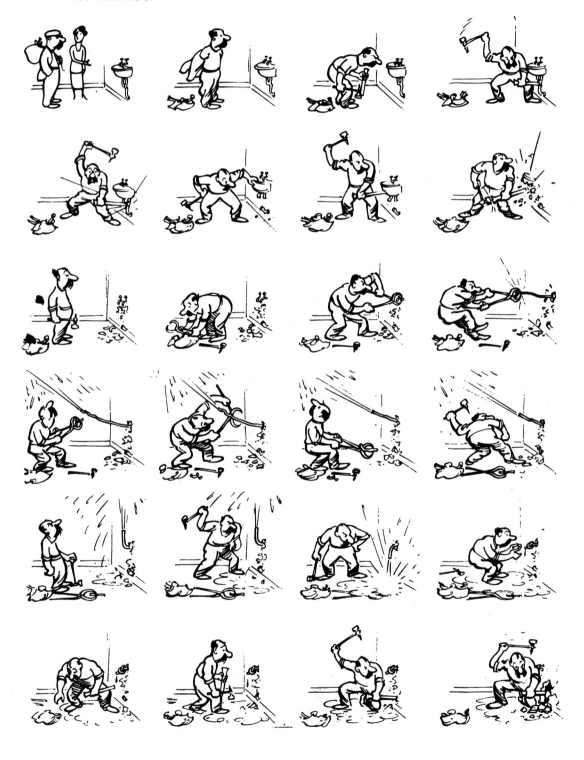

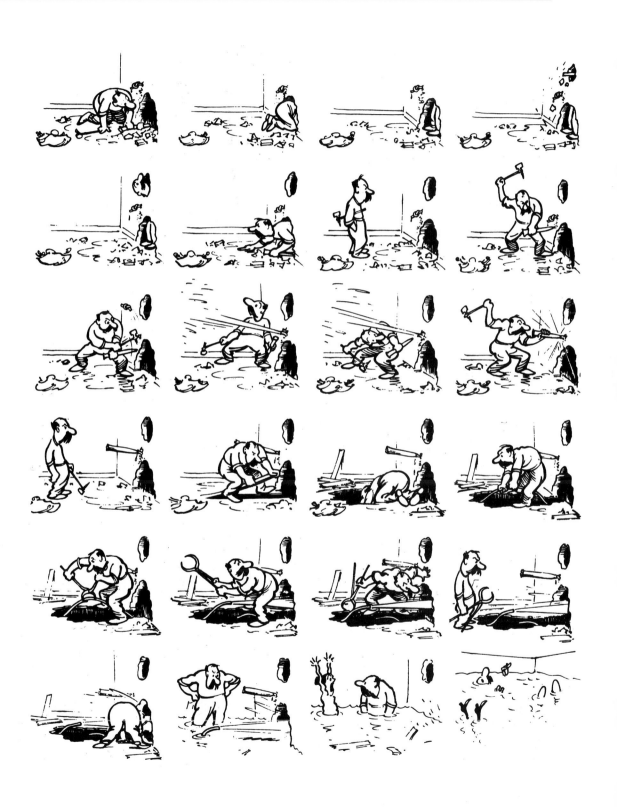

pictures by H.M. Bateman, from *The Man Who Drew the Twentieth Century*, edited by Michael Bateman

Read on!

1 This 'story' contains no words, but you can still 'read' it. How?
2 If it did not have a title, what clues are there to tell you what it is about?
3 If you had to divide this 'story' into sections such as 'beginning', 'middle' and 'end', where would you draw the lines and why?
4 Explain why the character behaves in the way he does in the various pictures. What clues are there? Copy the chart and make notes.

Clue	What it tells me about the behaviour of the character

5 Tell the 'story' briefly in the sequence of the pictures. Avoid using boring connectives such as 'then' and 'next'.

Write on!

1 Write the dialogue and narrative for the first four pictures. Use the Activity Sheet to help.
  - Write about each picture in a separate paragraph.
  - Look carefully at the situation, the characters and how you think they would speak, think and react.
  - How will you connect the four paragraphs? Avoid using words such as 'then' or 'next'.

2 Choose any one of the pictures on the Activity Sheet and think of a different outcome for the actions of the plumber. Write what would happen as a result of this in the story.
  - Think about how this would change the sequence of events in the story and therefore its ending.

Over to you!

1 Look carefully at the final picture. Tell the story in a longer form as a 'flashback': starting at the 'end' and explaining how you reached that position. You could start:

As I floated in the water, my nose nearly touching the ceiling, I thought back to my conversation earlier in the day, standing in the bathroom …

Use details about the situation and the character to make the story more than just a sequence of events. Dialogue helps. In this case it might be the plumber 'talking to himself'.

2 Another approach is to start in the middle of the story:

Just as I started to dig the hole deeper into the wall, I thought about how I had got myself into this situation …

Go back to the 'beginning' and show what led up to this 'picture'. Then tell the rest of the story:

I came out of my dream and got back to work. Nothing worse could happen. But I was wrong …

18 Making notes: charts and diagrams

Charts and diagrams can sometimes communicate information more effectively than plain text. The following text, chart and food web diagram (A) give information about food chains in and around an oak tree.

A Sparrow hawks and foxes eat small birds such as sparrows, robins and wood warblers. Foxes also eat squirrels. Sparrows eat insects such as the ladybird, four-spot carrion beetle and lacewing; both robins and wood warblers eat greenfly and lacewings; robins also eat ladybirds. Lacewings and ladybirds eat greenfly; four-spot carrion beetles eat caterpillars, such as the green oak roller. Greenfly eat the juices from leaves and caterpillars eat the leaves themselves.

Part of the food chain of an oak tree		
Animal or plant	**What it eats**	**What eats it**
leaves	The tree produces its own food	greenfly, green oak roller (moth) caterpillar
acorns	The tree produces its own food	squirrel
greenfly	leaves	ladybird, sparrow, robin, wood warbler, lacewing
green oak roller caterpillar	leaves	four-spot carrion beetle
ladybird	greenfly	robin, sparrow
four-spot carrion beetle	green oak roller caterpillar	sparrow
lacewing	greenfly	sparrow, robin, wood warbler
sparrow	greenfly, lacewing, ladybird, four-spot carrion beetle	sparrow hawk, fox
robin	ladybird, greenfly, lacewing	sparrow hawk, fox
wood warbler	greenfly, lacewing	sparrow hawk, fox
squirrel	acorns	fox
sparrow hawk	sparrow, robin, wood warbler	
fox	sparrow, robin, wood warbler, squirrel	

Making notes: charts and diagrams

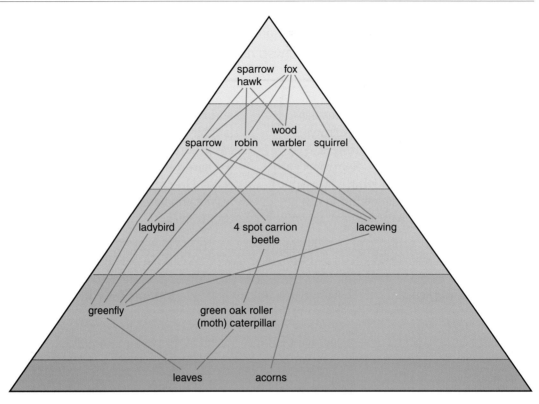

Part of the food web of an oak tree

B

The leaves and flowers of the rose bushes in the garden are curled and wilting and covered with aphids such as greenfly – all having a feast. Bluetits perch there pecking off the aphids. The lettuce have great holes in their leaves – eaten by slugs; I was glad to see a flock of thrushes landing and eating a hearty meal of fresh slugs. I don't mind the rabbits eating the grass, but I wish they'd leave the lettuce alone.

The scarecrow doesn't seem to stop the chaffinches and dormice eating the barley, but sparrowhawks swoop in and catch chaffinches and dormice. A fox slunk in today and caught a rabbit; it sometimes takes a dormouse or two as a snack (if the owl hasn't already eaten them).

Read on!

1 Look at A. Which do you find the most effective way in which to communicate the feeding habits of animals which visit or inhabit the oak tree: plain text, a chart or a diagram? Explain your answer.

2 Write some questions about the feeding habits of the animals which live on, or inhabit, the oak tree.

   Give them to a partner to answer.

3 Which animals or plants would be affected (and how) if the following became extinct:
   a) lacewing?
   b) squirrel?
   c) green oak roller moth?
   d) greenfly?

Write on!

1 Read the extract from a farmer's diary (B), which provides information about part of the food chain of a farm with a small garden. Make a chart to explain the food chain.

2 Draw a food web for the farm and the farmhouse garden.

Over to you!

Make notes about the feeding habits of animals in another habitat. Display your findings in the form of a chart and a food web. The Activity Sheet will help you to plan the food web.

19 Making notes: for and against

Opposite are the words of people interviewed in a radio programme discussing children's involvement in petty crime and vandalism, and whether one solution would be to have a 7 p.m. curfew for unaccompanied children under the age of twelve.

Hanna Carey

Professor Elizabeth James

Laura Woffle

WPC Ella Thomas

Tom Brown

Dennis Mennymoor

George Havagh-Mown

Dunstan Daire

Asma Agar

A

In order to learn to socialise, children need opportunities to talk to one another without any adults being present. Adults inhibit children's conversation. In our research we set topics for groups of eleven- to twelve-year-olds to discuss in groups of six, some with an adult chairing the discussion, some with one or more adults taking part, some with an adult observing and others with no adults present. We recorded the discussions and found that the discussions among the groups without adults were just as well organised and fair as those with adults, but the quality of the young people's contributions was higher: they were more open and spontaneous and the youngsters were not trying to 'give the right answers'. Where adults were present the youngsters tended to wait for them to lead and organise the discussion, but without adults they did this very effectively for themselves. They would have no opportunities for developing these social skills if they are supervised by adults during what is probably their only free time once their homework is done.

B

If they are not doing anything wrong, why should they object to being supervised?

C

If youngsters have plenty to do they don't get into trouble. What we need are good facilities for them: not for activities which the councillors think they want, but what they really want. We need to find this out from the youngsters – what kind of thing they want to do without having adults supervising their every move. Some young people would probably be able to help to organise events for themselves.

D

It would cut down petty crime in our town centre. Small shopkeepers are losing money through theft: you need eyes in the back of your head to see what these youngsters are up to. I'm not saying that all youngsters out on their own are up to no good, but some of them are, and they're the ones we want to stop.

G

Twelve-year-olds are capable of being responsible for their own safety and behaviour without having to be supervised by adults, *whatever* time of the day it is.

E

Parents have a legal responsibility for children of this age; they need not be with them all the time once they are old enough to be allowed some freedom, but they should check where they are and what they are doing.

F

Children under the age of twelve don't suddenly start behaving like monsters at 7 p.m.

J

Why should young people be discriminated against? Plenty of children under the age of twelve have a better sense of responsibility than some adults. There are many adults who are vandals, thieves and murderers.

H

We shouldn't have to put up with the noisy and loutish conduct of other people's children when our own are supervised and not allowed to behave like that.

I

I'm all for it. They lower the tone of the place: hanging around on the village green, dropping litter, charging about and shouting and swearing. The later it gets the worse they behave; drinking lager, dropping the cans everywhere – they get older ones to go in the off-licence for it. We used to enjoy a walk around the village on summer evenings until these louts ruined it. Where do their parents think they are and what do they think they are up to? That's what I want to know.

Read on!

1. Match the speech bubbles to the speakers. Explain why you matched them in this way.
2. Make a chart like this one and list the arguments which were given for and against a 7 p.m. curfew for children under the age of twelve:

For the curfew	Against the curfew

3. Did you think any of the quotations were biased? Explain why you think this is. Give examples from the texts. You could use a chart:

Biased quotations	Evidence

Write on!

Use the opinions in the text and any others you can think of to write an argument which either supports or disagrees with the proposal of a 7 p.m. curfew for anyone under the age of twelve who is not accompanied by an adult. The Activity Sheet helps you to organise your argument.

- Make it a balanced argument.
- List any opinions which oppose your views.

  Think of arguments against them. Write these arguments

Over to you!

Talk to people you know about an issue on which you have an opinion: for example, homework, pocket money, whether you should be paid for helping with jobs around your home or how animals or plants should be protected.

Make notes about their views. List them under headings 'For' and 'Against'. Plan an argument about the topic you have chosen. Use evidence to support your views. Argue against evidence which opposes them.

20 Persuasive language

A

OUR MOST EFFECTIVE AND BEST VALUE CLEANER

Aquamark

COMPLETELY PORTABLE

AS SEEN ON TV

BEFORE · AFTER

STEAM CLEANS ALL OVER THE HOME
- Carpets
- Curtains
- Upholstery
- Woodwork
- Windows
- Sinks
- Car Interiors
- Showers
- Ovens

Curtains/Upholstery

Ovens/Hobs

Tiles

Stairs

POWERFUL STREAM OF HOT AIR STEAMS OUT HARDENED STAINS

HAND HELD · LIGHTWEIGHT

STEAM CLEANER

"Cleans just about anything"

WITHOUT CHEMICALS OR SCRUBBING

Just how effective is steam cleaning? The revolutionary hand held Steam Cleaner operates at a temperature of about 130°F, a temperature that will dissolve dirt, grime, grease, oil from just about any surface throughout your home. Works on carpets, curtains, upholstery, tiles, windows, sinks, ovens, hobs, showers, baths, even car interiors. You can clean practically any room in your home with less fuss and without chemical cleaners!

Leaves glass, ceramic and enamel surfaces sparkling clean with no smears or film build-up as with normal household cleaners.

Steam Cleaning is the perfect solution to dust allergy sufferers - it reduces dust mite population. Regular steam cleaning helps destroy bacteria and fungus and prevent further re-infestation. Steam pillows, mattresses, duvets, carpets, curtains -

It's so simple you'll wonder why no-one thought of it before.

Once you've experienced the power of steam cleaning, we feel sure you won't want to use anything else again. The Steam Cleaner requires no chemicals or special additives just simply water straight from the tap. What could be cheaper or easier?

Perfect for steam ironing too! Suits, dresses, skirts, shirts - simply hold the unit close to the fabric and allow the steam to "melt" away the creases.

To order simply ring our credit card ordering service, anytime day or night, send a fax, email or complete the coupon and post to us today. If you are not completely satisfied, simply return within 30 days for a refund of the purchase price. Delivery is by Parcel Force on your behalf unless you instruct us otherwise by calling 0870 758 0002.

MasterCard/Visa/Switch/Delta/Solo Cards
Card Holders

0870 758 0001

24 HOUR, 7 DAY SERVICE
ORDERS ACCEPTED BY FAX
0870 750 0827
or email to orders@hhsuk.com

DRAMATICALLY REDUCES DUST MITES AND BACTERIA AROUND THE HOME

CLEANS

SANITISES

IRONS

Post Orders to: Health & Home Shopping, Dept 6009SL, 47 Brunel Avenue, Manchester M5 4JB
If you do not wish to receive mailings from other companies please write separately to Dept. NM at the above address.

A TOOL FOR EVERY JOB

The Hand Held Steam Cleaner has a see-through water tank and special attachments to tackle just about any and every cleaning job in and around the home.

Small brushes to cope with delicate fabrics, steamer nozzle for hard to reach places, larger brushes for larger areas of cleaning and two sizes of squeegee for windows, tiles, etc.

FOR ONLY

£49.95 + p&p

To Health & Home Shopping, Dept 6009SL, 47 Brunel Avenue, Manchester M5 4JB
Please send me

ITEM	PRICE	QTY	TOTAL
Aquamark Steam Cleaner With attachments	£49.95 + p&p		
Please add £2.95 p&p to entire order			£2.95
		GRAND TOTAL	

I enclose Cheque/P.O.(made payable to Health & Home Shopping) for £............... or charge my MasterCard/Visa/Switch/Delta/Solo Account.

My Card No. is .... Expiry Date .... Issue No. (Switch/Solo Cards)......

Name Mr/Mrs/Miss/Ms .... Address ....

.... Post Code ....

Tel. No. .... Email address ....

Please allow up to 28 days for delivery. Offer applies to UK mainland inc. N. Ireland only.

Health & Home Shopping Ltd. Co. Reg. No. 2933317

Persuasive language

B

Birdseye Chicken O's

The meat from which Chicken O's are made is 100% chicken breast. They are a rich source of protein. Not only will your children love their fun shape, but you will also know that you are giving them the nutrients they need. Did you know that a single serving of Chicken O's contains vital elements of a healthy diet for 7–10 year-olds? These include: 40% (RNi) of the daily requirement for protein (protein contains amino acids which are crucial for the growth and repair of your child's body); approximately a third of the RNi for the B vitamins thiamine and niacin (these release the energy from food which children need to grow and develop); more than a quarter of the RNi for phosphorus to help them to build strong bones and teeth; more than half the RNi for vitamin B6, which breaks down proteins and is needed for healthy blood; and 19% of the RNi for vitamin B12, which is needed to manufacture healthy red blood cells. Chicken O's are available in all major supermarkets.

Glossary

RNi Reference Nutrient intake, taken from *Dietary Reference Values for Food and Energy and Nutrients for the United Kingdom*, 1991

Read on!

1 What layout features does the advertisement (A) use to attract the reader's attention? Give examples from the advertisement.

Think about flashes, bullet points, headlines, fonts and the different sizes of print.

2 What important features of the vacuum cleaner does the advertisement stress? Support your answer by quoting from the text.

3 Is the language formal or informal? Give examples to support your answer.

4 How does the language of the advertisement attract the reader? Give examples of powerful or expressive:
   * adjectives
   * adverbs
   * verbs
   * phrases.

Write on!

1 Read the information in B, which is taken from an advertisement for Bird's Eye 'Chicken O's'. List the parts which you think should be highlighted as bullet points, stars, flashes or headlines.

2 Describe any pictures you would include in the advertisement.

3 In the advertisement, what would you emphasise, and why?

4 To which group or groups of people is the advertisement addressed? Explain your answer, and support it with examples from the text.

5 How would you alter the advertisement so that it would appeal to children aged about five to ten?

Think about:
* *attracting attention*
* *changing the formality of style*
* *changing the length of sentences*
* *simplifying the language*
* *summarising details.*

Over to you!

Plan an advertisement for something you have designed and made.
* Decide who your audience is.
* Think about how to make your advertisement appeal to this audience.
* Think of the key selling points.

* Decide what information should be included.

Use the Activity Sheet to plan your advertisement.

21 Speeches

In this extract, a group of boys is stranded on a desert island. When they start to argue, one party goes off to hunt, while the other stays behind to keep a fire lit as a rescue signal. One rule they have is that whoever holds a large shell (a conch) is the one who can speak to the entire group at a meeting.

Piggy held out his hands for the conch but Ralph shook his head. This speech was planned, point by point.

'We've all got to use the rocks again. This place is getting dirty.' He paused. The assembly, sensing a crisis, was tensely expectant. 'And then: about the fire.'

Ralph let out his spare breath with a little gasp that was echoed by his audience. Jack started to chip a piece of wood with his knife and whispered something to Robert, who looked away.

'The fire is the most important thing on the island. How can we ever be rescued except by luck, if we don't keep a fire going? Is a fire too much for us to make?'

He flung out an arm.

'Look at us! How many are we? And yet we can't keep a fire going to make smoke. Don't you understand? Can't you see we ought to – ought to die before we let the fire out?'

There was a self-conscious giggling among the hunters. Ralph turned on them passionately.

'You hunters! You can laugh! But I tell you the smoke is more important than the pig, however often you kill one. Do you all see?' He spread his arms wide and turned to the whole triangle. 'We've got to make smoke up there – or die.'

He paused, feeling for his next point.

'And another thing.'

Someone called out: 'Too many things.'

There came mutters of agreement. Ralph overrode them.

'And another thing. We nearly set the whole island on fire. And we waste time, rolling rocks, and making little cooking fires. Now I say this and make it a rule, because I'm chief. We won't have a fire anywhere but on the mountain. Ever.'

There was a row immediately. Boys stood up and shouted and Ralph shouted back.

'Because if you want a fire to cook fish or crab, you can jolly well go up the mountain. That way we'll be certain.'

Hands were reaching for the conch in the light of the setting sun. He held on and leapt on the trunk.

'All this I meant to say: Now I've said it. You voted me for chief. Now you do what I say.'

They quietened, slowly, and at last were seated again. Ralph dropped down and spoke in his ordinary voice.

'So remember. The rocks for a lavatory. Keep the fire going and smoke showing as a signal. Don't take fire from the mountain. Take your food up there.'

Jack stood up, scowling in the gloom. And held out his hands.

'I haven't finished yet.'

'But you've talked and talked!'

'I've got the conch.'

Jack sat down, grumbling.

'Then the last thing. This is what people can talk about.'

He waited till the platform was very still.

'Things are breaking up. I don't understand why. We began well; we were happy. And then…' He moved the conch gently, looking beyond them to nothing, remembering the beastie, the snake, the fire, the talk, the fear.

'Then people started getting frightened.'

A murmur, almost a moan, rose and passed away. Jack had stopped whittling. Ralph went on, abruptly.

'But that's littluns' talk. We'll get that straight. So the last part, the bit we can talk about, is kind of deciding on the fear.'

The hair was creeping into his eyes again.

'We've got to talk about this fear and decide there's nothing in it. I'm frightened myself sometimes; only that's nonsense! Like bogies. Then, when we've decided, we can start again and be careful about things like the fire.' A picture of three boys walking along the bright beach flitted through his mind. 'And be happy.'

Ceremonially, Ralph laid the conch on the trunk beside him as a sign that the speech was over.

from *Lord of the Flies* by William Golding

Read on!

1 What are the differences between a speech, a discussion and an argument?
2 How do you know that this is a speech?
3 'The speech was planned point by point'. Copy the chart and make a list of the points Ralph was trying to make:

Point he was making	How he tried to make it clearer

4 Making a speech is as much about the way you deliver it as the content. What kinds of thing does Ralph do when he speaks to make his points even stronger?
   - How does he use his body?
   - Why does he pause so much?
   - How does he use words?
5 One characteristic of speeches is the 'rhetorical question' – a question which does not really need an answer. It is asked and often repeated, for effect. Find some examples of these in the passage.

Write on!

1 Read the extract again and write a series of questions you would like to ask Ralph in response to his speech. What would you like clarifying or what faults can you see in his argument?
   - Who? What? Why? When? How?
2 Use these to write Jack's reply to the Ralph's 'points' in the same style as this extract. He is obviously opposed to

Ralph's views. What might he say? How might he say it to persuade the boys? Copy the chart and use it to help you:

Arguments		
How he might use his body		
Use of rhetorical questions		
The reactions of others		

Over to you!

Write your own speech to be delivered to the class, for example concerning an important environmental or sporting issue about which you feel strongly. Use the Activity Sheet to help you to make some notes:

- Plan the points you want to make – think about the sequence they should follow.
- What are you really trying to convince your audience about? Choose one or two main points.
- Find evidence to prove your points.
- Think about what language devices you might use to persuade your audience: rhetorical questions; repetition; pauses for effect; ways of connecting your points ... 'and another thing ...'; summarising the points you have already made – 'So remember ...'; short, punchy sentences.
- Use body language – point to emphasise certain points; raise your voice only when necessary – a speech should not be shouted; speak slowly and pause for effect; try to stand in a higher position than your audience.

22 Leaflets

A

Fantasy Fun

Enjoy the Cadbury Fantasy Factory - a light hearted look at chocolate making with help from Mr Cadbury's Parrot and the Bean Team . . . . a must for children of all ages!

Exclusive Chocolate Bargains..

. . . in the Chocolate Shop. Packed with all your favourite Cadbury chocolate, with souvenirs and gifts to suit everyone. There's the chance to buy the chocolates made by our demonstrators, plus exclusive offers and special bargains, available only at Cadbury World.

Tasty Treats

The Cadbury World Restaurant offers a selection of light snacks and drinks during opening hours. Hot lunch choices are available between 11am and 3pm when you can choose from a variety of fare including roasts, Dish of the Day and for children, our Mini Muncher Meal.

Discover More ...

. . . in the Cadbury Collection, a separate exhibition devoted to telling more of the Cadbury story and the history of the village of Bournville. The exhibition includes The Robert Opie Collection of Cadbury Packaging, "Sweet Delights" - a replica 1930s sweet shop and "The Bournville Story" archive film show. Situated at the rear of the building near the Children's Play Area, entrance to the Cadbury Collection is free.

Family Fun

Children will love the Play Area with its Creme Egg climbing frame. And there's a picnic area nearby so Mum and Dad can relax and watch the fun. Drinks and snacks are available from Chuckle Bean's Snack Bar near the Play Area and Cadbury Collection.

Chocolate Paradise

For anyone who loves chocolate, a visit to Cadbury World is a trip to paradise. It's a fabulous family experience all about chocolate - sights, sounds, smells and of course tastes!

See, smell and taste chocolate fresher than anywhere else. Watch our Demonstrators at work creating the Cadbury World range of chocolate products. And you can view a Cadbury Packaging Plant where bars of chocolate are wrapped and packed.*

*The Packaging Plant is open on most days but is subject to production restrictions and cannot be guaranteed to be open or to be operational. Please check on arrival.

Order your own chocolate Chuckle Bean plaque personalised with a chocolate message of your choice. Place your order when booking on 0121 451 4159.

Aztec Secrets

Stroll through Central American rain forests to see where cocoa was first grown. Sample the spicy drink of "chocolatl" and share the secret of its ingredients with Emperor Montezuma.

Follow the story of chocolate across Europe to Birmingham to discover how John Cadbury began using cocoa and how the famous Cadbury's Dairy Milk chocolate bar was created.

Learn how chocolate is made by Cadbury today and how we create some of our best known products.

Into the Blue

Travel into the deepest, darkest corners of the Cadbury universe to discover life on Planet Astros. Journey inside the blue planet to discover why Astros are so delicious they're doomed...

For a carefree visit

- FREE parking.
- Picnic and play areas.
- Disabled parking.
- Disabled access throughout except parts of the Packaging Plant - waiting area provided.
- Disabled toilets.
- Guide dogs welcome except in production areas.
- Baby changing room.
- Pushchair access except the Packaging Plant - waiting area provided.
- French literature available.

- Cadbury World gift vouchers available.
- Information on places to visit and accommodation is available from the Birmingham Visitor Information Centre on 0121 693 6300.
- Group Bookings- special discounts available for groups of 15 or more. Please ring for details.

CORPORATE HOSPITALITY
A unique chocolate event
Ring 0121 454 8585
for details

BIRTHDAY PARTIES
a speciality - phone
0121 451 4171
for details

Please Note:

- Cadbury World is not a tour of the Cadbury factory.
- The Creme Egg Cars are for display only.
- Average Cadbury World visit lasts 2¼ hours.
- Smoking is prohibited throughout Cadbury World, including the Restaurant.
- We regret a mail order retail service is not available.

- We cannot guarantee that the Packaging Plant will be working at any particular time.
- There is lift access to Cadabra and the Packaging Plant area.
- NB: An optional section of the Packaging Plant is on an upper floor. A waiting area is provided for visitors with mobility problems.

How to find us

Not to scale

Directions

From M42, Jct 2 follow brown & white tourist signs on A441/A4040 due North for 6 miles.

From M5, Jct 2 follow brown & white tourist signs on A4123/A4040.

From M5, Jct 4 follow brown & white tourist signs on A38/A4040 North East, 7 miles.

From M6, Jct 6 follow A38 Central & South/Bromsgrove to Selly Oak, then follow brown & white tourist signs for 7 miles.

BUS AND TRAIN

From City centre take bus numbers 83, 84 or 85 to Bournville.
From Bournville Railway Station - follow Cadbury World fingerposts and wall signs.
From the Birmingham and Worcester Canal and Bournville Railway Station (disabled access) - exit by ramps at the South end of the station, turn right (car park on right) for approx. 150m. Turn right into Franklin Way. At end of Franklin Way cross Bournville Lane and turn left. From here follow Cadbury World fingerposts and wall signs.

Parts of a leaflet about Cadbury World

B

The castle is reached by a steep footpath or a staircase with 65 steps. It is open every day except 24–26 December. Pre-booked groups from schools are welcome. There are discounts for groups of 10 or more. There are facilities for changing babies. There is a shop which sells sweets, souvenirs and camera films. There is wheelchair access to the ground floor only, with a reduced entry fee and free entry for a companion. To get there by road, take the M42 and leave it at Junction 12 (A5). Take the first turning on the right and continue to the castle entrance on the left. It is a magnificent motte and bailey castle. There is a restaurant with seating for up to 40 people. Opening hours are from 9.00 a.m. to 5.00 p.m. daily, except for Sundays (10.00 a.m. to 4.00 p.m.). The castle dates from the 12th century. The tower bedroom is said to be haunted by the ghost of a woman who died in the 15th century. The admission charge for adults is £4.00 and for children £2.00. There are toilet facilities for people with limited mobility. Inside the medieval fortress are Tudor and Jacobean buildings. The nearest station is Tamworth. A sign there gives directions to the castle via a footpath. The walk takes about 10 minutes. There is a reduced entrance fee of £2.00 for senior citizens. There is no charge for under-fives. The Norman Exhibitions feature models of the castle and its inhabitants as they were then, including the prisoners in the dungeons.

Read on!

1 How does the Cadbury World leaflet (A) appeal to different audiences? Copy and complete the chart:

Group of people	Evidence
Very young children	
Older children	
Teenagers	
Young adults	
Elderly people	
Other adults	
Schools	

Think about the features included in the leaflet, the pictures and the cartoon characters.

2 Evaluate the leaflet. How well does it inform people? Copy and complete the chart.

Informing people	+	=	–	Example
About what they can see and do				
About when to visit				
About how to get to Cadbury World				

Key
+ very well   = fairly well   – not very well

3 List the words which are used to make Cadbury World sound interesting.

Write on!

1 Think of a way in which to organise the information in B as a leaflet in which people can find the information they need.

Begin by making notes on separate pieces of paper or on a chart of any pieces of information which could be grouped together. Write headings for each section.

2 Write a leaflet about the castle.

Over to you!

Design a leaflet to attract primary school children to another place you know.

Use the Activity Sheet to help you to plan your leaflet.